A PASSION FOR ART

A PASSION FOR ART

Art Collectors and their Houses

IRENE GLUDOWACZ
SUSANNE VAN HAGEN
PHILLIPE CHANCEL

FOREWORD BY PIERRE BERGÉ
WITH 208 ILLUSTRATIONS IN COLOUR

Thames & Hudson

Contents

What makes a great collector?

At school we collect good or bad grades, later we collect lovers or mistresses, and sometimes we collect parking tickets and speeding fines. But presumably, none of these turn us into collectors. The dictionary informs us that a collection is a set of objects gathered together for their beauty or value. But is this right? In my opinion, such a definition misrepresents the mind of the collector, his or her obsession, persistence, phobia even. I know some people who collect corks that are neither beautiful nor valuable, and others who go for matchboxes, of which the same can be said. Collectors devote their lives to their passion, and sacrifice almost everything to it. If, after many years, they decide to send it to auction, it's more out of vanity than financial considerations. And generally they will start collecting something else. An object on its own can reflect an interest; two objects make a pair; but with three, you have started a collection. And then you will use every available means to expand it. But you need time, patience and cunning to achieve your ends, as well as knowledge and experience, for true collectors are every bit as competent as most professionals in their field.

You must also pass on this virus as soon as possible to your children. Collecting postage stamps, for example, remains one of the finest journeys a child can undertake. Who can fail to admire the beauty and mystery of those stamps that have reached us from the ends of the earth? And what child can ever forget those marvellous first moments of exploration?

Some people might say that certain collections are boring. But who cares? What matters is the enthusiasm of the collector, the emotion that is experienced when the longed-for object finally, deliriously, comes into the predestined possession of its seeker. To collect is first and foremost to love; and love is all you need.

Pierre Bergé
Fondation Pierre Bergé et Yves Saint Laurent

Giuliano Gori
NATURE IN ART OR ART IN NATURE

As the head of a very old Tuscan family that has lived in the Italian city of Prato in Tuscany since the 15th century, Giuliano Gori has run a textile business, in keeping with local tradition. He is, however, equally well known for the passion that has led him to assemble a collection of contemporary art, specifically created for the huge park surrounding his late-17th-century villa which is situated in the village of Santomato, in the hills between Prato and Pistoia.

As attached to his family as he is to the land, Gori has passed on his passion to his four children, nephews and twelve grandchildren, who appear equally committed to the continuation of his collection.

It was purely by chance, when Gori was still a young man, just after the Second World War, that he discovered art for the first time in the studio of a local painter called Gino Fanciullacci. He fell in love with the colours of the paintings, so typical of Tuscany, and he wanted to buy one. The artist would have given it to him as a present, but he insisted on paying, feeling it

would be wrong to start a collection without spending his money. It was the first of many purchases that would bring together some of the greatest names in 20th-century art: Picasso, Braque, Léger, Bacon, Lichtenstein, Warhol, as well as Burri, Fontana, Klein, Arman and César. There is nothing impersonal in this collection of names, however. In almost every case, they are linked to memorable meetings with the artists themselves, many of whom have visited his home, and to whose work he has remained loyal, regarding the purchase of their art almost as a religious rite.

He has the deepest respect for the creative act, and recalls that in 1961 he was particularly impressed when he visited a museum of ancient art in Spain, where he saw works being restored in the context in which they were first painted. 'Seeing this', he says, 'made me understand the importance of the site for which a work is created, in comparison to a work that is made in a studio, to be taken elsewhere.' This discovery was crucial to him, and led to a fundamental change in his approach to collecting.

In this spirit, he sought to revive the Renaissance tradition whereby artists were offered a particular space

LEFT In the front garden of the Villa Celle, Roberto Barni's bronze sculpture *Silent Servants* (Servi Muti), 1988.

ABOVE Giuliano Gori.

11

in which to create a work that would harmonize with its environment. Thanks to a meeting with Amnon Barzel, who had already promoted this kind of art in Israel, and would later become Director of the Pecci Museum of Contemporary Art in Prato, he was able to put his idea into operation.

In the 1950s, being a man accustomed to action rather than words, Giuliano Gori had already devoted his first house to art. In the spring of 1970, he bought the Villa Celle, where he was able to develop the programme that he describes as 'arte ambientale', or site-specific art. 'If we live like princes, it's not because we have chosen this way of life for our own sake, but because we want to give life to a collection.'

The Fattoria di Celle (Celle Farm) was built by Cardinal Carlo Agostino Fabroni, a patron of the arts, at the end of the 17th century, and is one of the finest examples of architecture from that period. The main house has an adjoining chapel, a farm and an Italian garden that surrounds the villa and slopes down into the landscape. The surrounding park opens onto a wood and an olive grove, and if you follow

the various paths, you will come to a waterfall and a small lake that are among the features of this estate which spans forty-five hectares, and also houses sculptures by artists of international standing. It would take you at least four hours to cover this vast area, to see for yourself the works that have been specially commissioned for this enchanted place. Not only do they fit in with the natural environment, they actually enhance it, and in turn are enhanced by it, through an interaction of pure symbiosis.

This form of art has become extremely rare in our time, and artists are no longer accustomed to working on this type of commission. But the experience has been rewarding for those who have been prepared to accept the constraints. Richard Serra, for example, was flexible enough to abandon steel, his favourite material, in favour of Tuscan stone. The Polish artist Magdalena Abakanowicz, similarly, had for a while convinced herself that the 'bronze age' was over and that she must make her way with concrete, resin and marble. But for *Katarsis*, the work she created for the park at Celle, she returned to this noble metal and has remained faithful to it ever since.

Gori does not confine himself to offering these artists a space. He also opens up new territories for their art, which they might not have discovered for themselves. One memorable instance involved the French artists Anne and Patrick Poirier, who had previously only worked indoors and were quite convinced that they could not create anything elsewhere. Gori commissioned a piece from them because he knew their history and their work, which is based on Etruscan traditions and Greek mythology. He persuaded them to conquer their doubts, and they chose a space at the bottom of a little waterfall, where they devised an extraordinary piece. They sculpted and transported to the site a stone that was like a mythical Greek figure, and set up lances around it, bearing quotations from the poet Virgil. Recently the Poiriers, speaking at a conference in Bologna , stated that Gori had changed their lives twenty years before by commissioning them to do the first in what became an extensive series of works situated in the landscape, worldwide.

In site-specific art, the artist may appear to have a great deal of freedom, but in fact the scope of the work is limited by the constraints imposed by the natural environment. Giuliano Gori takes great care to protect the park that surrounds his villa, and everything must be scrupulously conserved: the landscape must remain intact, no tree may be cut down, no stone displaced. He has put into practice a favourite doctrine of his friend, the Italian art critic Carlo Belli: 'The rights of art begin where those of nature end.' This might be the motto of the Fattoria di Celle. Such principles are all the more necessary because the natural world is constantly changing, and conservation must also take into account the seasons and vagaries of the weather. The estate is under the permanent supervision of a team of university researchers and botanists.

Beyond the boundaries of this protected area, however, artists are more free to explore their ideas, and are encouraged to seek out their ideal space. The best example of this approach is the American artist Alan Sonfist who, during his search for the most suitable spot, came across a large and unusual circular space within the olive grove. With the help of searchers,

15

he found out which plants had been the first to grow there in ancient times, and then he sought to put these plants back into the round space among the olive trees. In the wood, he photographed some branches that fallen from the trees, without touching them, and then he made bronze replicas of them. He placed these six bronze branches around the plants, making them into guardians of a sacred forest, surrounded by the laurel that also encircled the shrine to Apollo in ancient Greece. For the Romans, laurel symbolized peace after victory, and formed the garlands with which heroes were honoured. As an entrance to 'the poet's house' and then to the sacred forest, the artist constructed an arch, and one must lower one's head before stepping inside. In addition, around the laurel, Sonfist placed a circle of special stones which are known to conserve heat: these can only be found on Tuscan soil and are essential for the vines which are used in the making of Chianti wine. This workis completed by a circle of olive trees and a crown of wheat: each year the wheat has to be planted again so that the work can keep its shape. In this way, it has to pass through the stages that are linked to the land: the wheat equals bread, the olive trees stand for olive oil, the Chianti stones represent wine, antiquity and poetry are represented by the laurel, and finally the protected garden stands for the sacred forest.

Site-specific art is a form that normally finds expression in the external environment, but this is not always the case. Some artists have created works that incorporate parts of the villa itself, where they work *in situ*. Gori again lets them choose a location, so that they can devise a piece that will be in harmony with the architecture, such as *Camera di San Francesco* by Nicola de Maria.

ABOVE The dining room of the Villa Celle. *The Hairpins* by Alexander Calder can be seen in the corner. To the right of this sculpture is Joan Miró's *Woman, Bird, Stars* (Femme, oiseau, étoiles), 1942; to the left is Giacomo Balla's *Figure + Landscape* (Figura + paesaggio), 1916.

16

Most of the artists invited by the Gori family to create works have also become personal friends. Each stays in the villa for several months, inevitably forming a relationship with the patron; but more than that, the mutual trust and close cooperation that the work involves usually culminate in a bond of friendship. Major collectors and curators also go to the Villa Celle, where it is a point of honour for the Goris to bring art lovers together, and every year to open their estate to visitors, who can see the collection by appointment, free of charge.

Today, the most important part of the collection however is not inside the house, and does not comprise the works of acknowledged masters or what Gori calls his 'historical collection'. He still purchases works, through friends or as a result of meeting artists, but he stopped 'playing the collector,' as he puts it, in the 1970s, preferring to lend out his works for exhibitions in museums and galleries, mainly in Italy and the rest of Europe. Though his collection began with these 'historical' works, its continuation lies in the bold, site-specific pieces.

The collection and creative programme are at the very centre of Gori's life and that of his family, and it makes him proud to know that these works will always remain there. In the same spirit, he does not want the paintings and sculptures to be scattered after his death, or for people to fight or haggle over them. He wants them to remain in the family, and expects his children and grandchildren to make sacrifices for this purpose: they do so willingly, it seems, as they too are caught up in the passion which drives the master of the house. Most are now collectors and art lovers in their own right, and his wife too has devoted her life to art. One day, when he offered her jewelry, she responded quite simply by saying that she would prefer a painting.

ABOVE Dominating the little study is Francis Bacons's *Study for a Portrait*.

17

The Gori Collection at the Fattoria di Celle has acquired an international reputation, having given birth to, and developed a unique artistic experience; and it has spawned a number of imitators. As the pioneer of this 'arte ambientale', Gori is often invited to pass on his knowledge by supervising similar projects, for instance at the hospital in Pistoia. He is generous with his time and expertise, even displaying his collection abroad by means of one hundred and forty crates full of models, drawings, sketches and documents relating to his works. In recent times, four major Japanese museums have devoted their space to the collection, as have numerous museums in Europe, and a tour of the United States is scheduled for 2006.

Gori does not wish to be known as an art patron, even less as a collector. He calls himself 'a non-profit-making entrepreneur', but he is certainly a fine example of those patrons once common in the Renaissance, offering a home to artists and commissioning works, for their own pleasure, and ultimately for the love of art itself.

LEFT *The Death of Ephialtes* (La mort d'Ephialtes), 1982, marble and bronze, by Anne and Patrick Poirier, in the garden of the villa.

DOUBLE PAGE OVERLEAF
Melencolia II, 2002, by Robert Morris and Claudio Parmiggiani.

19

Ulla and Heiner Pietzsch
FREINDS OF MAX ERNST

Just after the Second World War, in 1946, Heiner Pietzsch discovered modern art amid the ruins of his home city of Dresden. At the age of sixteen, he went on a school trip to see an exhibition organized by the historian Will Grohmann, whom he was later to meet many times. The event was an eye-opener for everyone, as it showed the scale of the systematic art censorship exercised by the Nazis. Pietzsch learned what was meant by the Nazi expression 'degenerate art'. For the first time in many years, those artists who had been condemned as 'degenerate' were presented to a public that was astonished by what they saw: the greatest modern artists, including the German Expressionists and Surrealists, including Max Ernst. A few years later, Pietzsch would become the most ardent collector of his works. The Grohmann exhibition marked the beginning of his fascination with this type of art.

In 1955 he moved from East to West Berlin. A few years later, he set up a company producing and marketing plastics. He already knew Ulla, and

LEFT A view of the garden. In the foreground, on the left, is the sculpture *Two arcs of 240⁰* (Zwei Bögen von 2400), 1995, by Bernard Venet.

ABOVE RIGHT Ulla and Heiner Pietzsch in front of Paul Delvaux's painting *The Meeting* (La Rencontre), 1942.

after their marriage in 1956 she too moved to West Berlin, where their shared interest in art led them to make their first purchases of modern paintings; though in those early days, as they now recall with some amusement, their main aim was to decorate their house! Their first acquisition was Gerhard Altenbourg's *The Swing*. After a few years, however, they decided not to buy pictures simply on a whim, but to assemble a proper collection. Various journeys, visits to international exhibitions, and also discussions and exchanges with friends contributed to decisions that took them from one art world into another. Their tastes also developed: Ulla loved the Surrealists, while Heiner was more interested in Abstract Expressionism and the new generation of post-war American artists.

Surrealism, the movement which emerged in the 1920s under the leadership of poet and writer André Breton, was both fascinating and complex. It touched on all creative processes, using psychic forces that had been freed from the controlling powers of reason. In painting, the movement gave rise to some great artists, all of whom are represented in the Pietzsch Collection, mostly from 1920 to 1940. Max Ernst is the most

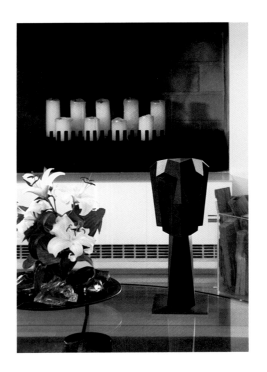

prominent among those represented, with major works such as *Painting for Young People* (1943), painted in Sedona, Arizona. René Magritte's famous *Magician's Accomplices* (1926) is there too, alongside works by Yves Tanguy, Salvador Dalí and Paul Delvaux. The couple also acquired paintings by lesser-known Surrealists such as Esteban Frances and Wolfgang Paalen. They are patient collectors and have been prepared to wait for years in order to acquire key Surrealist works, or those by great artists who only flirted with Surrealism, such as Pablo Picasso, Joan Miró and Jean Arp, whose reliefs reflect the concerns of Surrealism, as well as numerous other important figures in the history of 20th-century art, including the sculptors Alberto Giacometti, Alexander Calder, Jacques Lipchitz and Henri Laurens.

ABOVE LEFT Hans Uhlmann's *Female Head* (Weiblicher Kopf), 1940, in front of the fireplace.

ABOVE RIGHT Sculpture fragments, *Capricorn, 5 Fragments*, 1948, by Max Ernst.

OPPOSITE The large drawing room. Hanging from the ceiling is a mobile by Alexander Calder, *Hooded Man* (Le Cagoulard), 1953. On the left-hand wall is André Masson's *Massacre*, 1931; above the sofa is Victor Brauner's *Person on the Beach* (Personnage sur le plage), 1955; and to the right is Joan Miró's *Seated Woman* (Femme assise), 1935. The gallery is dominated by Paul Devaux's *The Meeting* (La Rencontre), 1942, which is situated next to *The Alarm* (L'Alerte), 1938, by Salvador Dalí.

A meeting with Max Ernst proved to be a turning point in the lives of Ulla and Heiner Pietzsch. It was at an exhibition in the Sprengel Museum in Hanover, in 1972, that they were captivated by this master of Surrealism – especially Ulla, who was fascinated by the man himself, his charisma, the intensity of his gaze, his extraordinarily sensitive view of the world, and his sense of humour which was perfectly in tune with her own. From that moment there could be no doubt that the work of Max Ernst would occupy a significant place in their continually expanding collection. There have even been occasions when Heiner himself has acted as a guide at various exhibitions of his favourite artist, and curators and experts alike have been amazed by the remarkable competence of the collector.

One of the couple's happiest memories concerns the acquisition of important sculptures by Ernst from the famous group entitled *Capricorn*. They were greatly assisted by Dallas, the artist's daughter-in-law, who was only too pleased to know that these works would find a good home in the prestigious collection of a couple who both loved and understood their creator. Thanks to this meeting, they also acquired drawings by Max

Ernst's son Jimmy, in an Abstract Expressionist style.

This brings us to the second major element of the collection, superbly represented by the violent expressiveness of post-war American artists – a passion that was reignited in 1988 when Heiner saw an exhibition at an outpost of New York's Whitney Museum. The Pietzsch Collection contains works by Pollock, Motherwell, Gorky, Rothko, Tobey, Gottlieb, Baziotes and Sam Francis – important pieces from the 1940s which demonstrate the extraordinary power of this American school that emerged from the Second World War, as well as the spontaneous interaction between the New York artists and the Europeans in exile: Ernst, Masson, Dalí, Duchamp and Lam. The Surrealist melting-pot had a potent effect on the young Americans, who initially even called themselves the 'abstract Surrealists', and the automatism and energy of this movement opened up new fields which soon imposed themselves on the world at large. In this context, the ambitious Pietzsch Collection constitutes a meeting point between the two continents, where the values of each receive equal respect, although it is Surrealism that has continued to dominate and to further enrich the collection.

Heiner is now spending less and less time on his professional career, in order to devote himself entirely to his passion, with Ulla as his faithful accomplice. They commute between New York and Berlin, where in 1988 they built a sophisticated 'cube' on the beautiful shores of the lake. Known as 'the white villa', it was specially constructed for their collection, designed in collaboration with the architect to provide the best possible setting for the works in terms of placement, lighting and even the dimensions of the walls. Here is a world tailored to their personal tastes and whims. In Ulla's room, for example, there are works by various women artists, especially Surrealists, and her husband believes that these denote love at first sight: works by Leonor Fini, Dorothea Tanning, Tamara de Lempicka and Elena Liessner-Blomberg.

The couple make the most of their collection, and have recently made some generous loans to the Residenzschloss in Dresden. They also belong to

LEFT A sculpture entitled *The Pitchfork* (La Fourche) by Joan Miró. Next to this is André Masson's painting *Narcissus* (Narcisse), 1937. On the table in the foreground is the sculpture *The Banner* (La Banderole), 1931, by Henri Laurens.

various groups of 'Friends' who support museums such as the Kunstsammlung Nordrhein Westphalen in Düsseldorf, and the National Gallery in Berlin, of which Heiner is one of the seven founders.

For Ulla, collecting is a matter of sensitivity, intuition and passion. Either she responds to a work or it leaves her cold, but whether or not to purchase is always a joint decision. What marks the exceptional quality of the Pietzsch Collection is ultimately a sense of deepening. It has developed with exemplary consistency. The couple began with a love of Surrealism, together with a passion for post-war American Abstract Expressionism, which also emphasized human subjectivity, fantasy and the subconscious. They remained faithful to their first Surrealist loves, and from the 1970s proceeded to focus on them, as though that first sight, when they encountered the work of Max Ernst, had been the most accurate, the one that showed them their true path. Their loyalty to Surrealism extends to the fact that even now they are supplementing their collection with photographic portraits of the artists, taken by Man Ray and Henri Cartier-Bresson.

There are no absolute boundaries to this subject matter, and the couple insist that no collection can ever be complete. One must know how to look, choose and buy works, even reselling items that are not essential to the collection. It is perseverance and passion that finally determine the exceptional coherence which has put the prestigious and attractive Pietzsch Collection at the forefront of the international art world. Although, as Heiner himself admits with a twinkle in his eye, art collecting is dangerous, not for one's health, but for one's wallet!

OPPOSITE Francis Bacons's monumental painting *Two Studies of the Human Body*, 1975. In front of this is the sculpture *The Awakening* (L'éveil) by Henri Laurens.

28

Ingvild Goetz
COMMITTED TO ART

Ingvild Goetz is a collector and a committed patron.
She was born in West Prussia, grew up in Hamburg,
and today lives with her family in Munich. Orginally
she wanted to be an artist, to study at the fine arts
academy in Munich, but her parents did not encourage
this interest in art because they felt that, coming from
a family of entrepreneurs, she should learn a more
traditional trade. At the age of twenty-four, however,
she married and began to paint. But having joined a
group of artists, she realized that her talent was at best
only mediocre, and so she decided instead to set up a
publishing firm to promote the work of young German
graphic artists. She began to make a lot of contacts,
travelling widely to see exhibitions and to train her eye.
She always sought to surround herself with work of the
highest quality, and the programme of her publishing
firm offered ample evidence of this, including works
by major artists such as Dieter Roth and Wolf Vostell.

Subsequently, she resolved
to open a gallery in
Zürich. Since she still
knew comparatively little
about the business, she

LEFT The collector on the
ground floor of her house.

DOUBLE PAGE OVERLEAF
The museum housing the Goetz
Collection, by Herzog & de
Meuron, completed in 1993.

31

decided to go to New York for six weeks, for the city had by then become a major centre for art. At that moment, a chance meeting resulted in a decisive influence on her career as a gallery owner. On the plane she met Harald Szeemann, who at that time was preparing the famous Kassel Documenta arts festival in Germany, together with Jean-Christophe Ammann. As she admits today, she owes an enormous debt to him.

Quite spontaneously, on their arrival in New York, Szeemann took the young gallery owner to various studios where she met some of the most famous artists of the time: Andy Warhol, Christo, Brice Marden, Eva Hesse, Robert Ryman and Sol LeWitt. During her first few visits, however, their work meant very little to her, because the art she had seen in Germany was so different to that in New York, which included the Minimalism of Marden and Ryman. Her thoughts began to change and after a little while she became receptive to the individualistic approaches of these different artists.

The two curators had

little difficulty in persuading their young recruit to join them on a trip to the west coast of America, where she accompanied them to the studios of Vija Celmins, Robert Irving and Ed Ruscha. Excited by all these contacts in New York and Los Angeles, Ingvild Goetz decided to organize an exhibition for some of them at the gallery she was planning to open in Zürich. In her enthusiasm and inexperience, however, she did not realize that some of these artists were already represented by dealers in the German-speaking countries, and subsequently discovered the scale of their dissatisfaction, which was thoroughly justified. She came to understand that the unique and often fraught relations between artists and gallery owners are vitally important, as they would indeed be for Goetz herself, in her own approach as a gallery owner.

In 1969, she opened her Zürich gallery with a political Happening, by the radical German artist Wolf Vostell, causing a scandal among the somewhat conventional Swiss. The artist's work, which attacked Swiss society for supplying arms to Angola, aroused such fierce hostility that in 1971 she was forced to close the gallery.

Goetz then left for Munich, where she opened a new gallery. She was one of the first female gallery owners in Germany, and began by exhibiting Italian Arte Povera. These works were to form the basis of her own private collection. It was a movement that was opposed to the increasingly technological modern world and set out to use the most elementary materials and creative techniques in order to convey a simple, poetic message.

Goetz was fascinated by Arte Povera, even though at that time Pop Art and Minimalism were the movements in vogue. She did also occasionally exhibit American artists such as Andy Warhol, Robert Rauschenberg, Sol LeWitt and Brice Marden, all of whom she had met during her first trip to New York; but more importantly, she was the first and only gallery owner in Germany at that time to support Spanish artists such as Antoni Tàpies and Chillida, the French Nouveau Réaliste Arman, and his fellow artist Christo, who wrapped her gallery in Munich.

Although she enjoyed running the gallery, especially meeting and working with the artists, increasingly she felt compelled to form

ABOVE Dining room with light box entitled *Restoration*, 1993/94, by Jeff Wall.

her own collection, instead of constantly having to part with works that she herself would have liked to keep. But the only way to do this was to stop showing them to clients. The result of this inner conflict was an uneasy balance between her work as a dealer and her passion as an art lover.

The situation was finally resolved in 1984, when she decided to close the gallery and devote herself entirely to collecting. By this time she was very experienced, and set about her task methodically, concentrating on socio-critical art which expressed the preoccupations of a particular generation. Arte Povera is one of the major features in her collection, which has gained international recognition as one of the most important specialist collections in the world, with exhibitions in Germany, Austria, Sweden and the United States. It has developed, in accordance with the times and the individual artists, from radical political awareness to personal and even marginal attitudes, expressed through a wide variety of media. As bold as ever, Goetz has acquired works that form a coherent whole, including film and video, from artists who now comprise the third generation since Arte Povera. Stan

Douglas, Rodney Graham, Doug Aitken, William Kentrige and Sam Taylor-Wood, as well as photographic artists such as Jeff Wall and Cindy Sherman. Nam Goldin and Thomas Demand are also represented, as are the installations of Sarah Lucas, Mona Hatoum and Andrea Zittel, the paintings of Karen Kilimnik and Jonathan Lasker, and various works on paper – her first love, which formed the beginning of her collection.

In 1989, Ingvild Goetz and her husband began to plan the construction of their own museum to house the collection, and in 1993 they commissioned the architects Herzog & de Meuron to build it. Thus they fulfilled Ingrid's long-standing desire to run her own museum, with its own structure and collection, to be organized according to her own principles. This is one of the very first private museums in Germany, and Ingrid holds two exhibitions a year. A staff of eight is employed to carry out the daily tasks necessary in a museum that is now famous for its two thousand works, some of which are willingly lent out to exhibitions elsewhere.

As Goetz herself says, the museum quickly became her teacher, obliging her to think carefully about future acquisitions and how to exhibit them. She has never departed from her own strict criteria, or from the parameters within which she makes her selections. She does not attend every art fair, only those she considers to be of major importance. Similarly, she favours the most well-known international galleries and, above all, as she has done from the start, she likes to be in personal contact with the artists whose work interests her. Consequently, this popular collector is always kept well-informed by those who are up to date with all the most important new developments. In addition, she reads all the specialist art magazines and, in the evenings, when the museum has closed its doors, she devours the latest catalogues.

After forty years on the international art scene, Ingvild Goetz has witnessed a good deal of repetition, whenever there is a shortage of new forms, especially in the field of painting. Nevertheless, her personal enthusiasm always keeps heron the alert for original messages conveyed by the present generation of artists, no matter how easy or difficult they are to decipher.

She has sufficient confidence in her own judgment to make her decisions unaided, after initially finding out all she can, and she only consults her husband, himself a collector, when she has to choose between several works by the same artist. For instance, he assisted her when she wanted to buy a work by Matthew Barney, the last of five films in the *Cremaster Cycle*, which was very expensive but completed a coherent ensemble by one of the most important artists of the 1990s.

It is easy to see why major museums are anxious to involve Goetz when it comes to new acquisitions, all the more so since she only complies when she knows that there is an active role for her to play. She is a member of the Museum of Modern Art (MoMA) in New York, and is on the committee of its department for works on paper, which she supports by donating pieces by German artists. It is an extremely interesting contact for both parties. She is also generous with gifts of works that no longer fit into the context of her collection. Museums in Germany, such as those of Magdeburg and

Dresden, which are not rich enough to afford new acquisitions, have benefited from her generosity.

Throughout her life Goetz has shown that, if a work of art is the setting for an artist's communion with his or her inner self, so the collector in turn seeks to visualize his or her own work of art by appropriating that of another. The resulting credo is one of infinite richness, creating a dialogue through which one can learn a great deal about the art of collecting, as well as about oneself. As for the actual artwork, it emanates from the artist but, having once become the property of the collector, it becomes a part of his or her creation. This is a belief beyond doubt in the mind of Goetz, who stands at the forefront of contemporary art, regarded by many as a trend-setter. And she remains as innovative and youthful in spirit as ever.

First a gallery owner, then a collector, Goetz began by wanting to be an artist herself. She has remained at the heart of the artistic world by becoming a collector who is always in tune with the times, succeeding in creating an original world, within the world of art, that is indeed her own, and where she lives and shares her passion with a generosity that is all too rare.

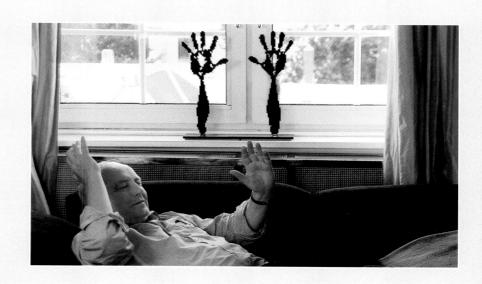

Harald Falckenberg
PIONEER OF CONTEMPORARY ART

Harald Falckenberg is a generous, extremely active pioneer of international renown in the field of contemporary socio-critical art. He runs a family company in the oil industry and is also an honorary judge at the constitutional court in Hamburg.

From the beginning, he showed a precocious entrepreneurial talent. Falckenberg comes from a Hamburg family with a long commercial tradition. After studying law in Berlin, Hamburg, Freiburg and the United States, he founded a private law school in Hamburg to prepare students for their examinations, before pursuing his successful career in the business world and at the constitutional court.

For ten years now he has been one of the most visible collectors on the contemporary international art scene, amassing more than one thousand five hundred works. But Harald Falckenberg is not the sort of man who simply sets out methodically and systematically to acquire works of art; he is also at pains to forge links with the artists, with exhibition organizers, and with the public at large. Each year since he began, he has devoted more and more of his finances to contemporary art, which is truly a passion. He is constantly on a quest to learn more about others and about himself, and even though this pursuit is shared and savoured by all collectors, he more than most has come to value the experience of other people.

It was in fact an artist-friend in Hamburg, Petrus Wandrey, who first kindled his desire to become an art collector. He became president of the Hamburg Kunstverein and, together with another friend, Hans Jochen Waitz, created a foundation at the Hamburger Kunsthalle which makes permanent loans of contemporary artworks.

His own collection, however, focuses mainly on international contemporary art, sometimes on young artists and also on those who work around Hamburg. Contact with the local art scene has been vitally important to him from the very start, and he has never forgotten this, even today. His frequent trips to

LEFT Staircase with mural *Black Stroke 3*, 1995, by Petrus Wandrey; on the right, a neon installation by Dan Flavin, 1996.

ABOVE RIGHT Harald Falckenberg at the window, in front of the sculpture *Touch 3/3*, 1996, by Petrus Wandrey.

DOUBLE PAGE OVERLEAF Drawing room with picture by C. O. Paeffgen, *Bühl Heights* (Bühler Höh), 1991, and Gerhard Richter's *Röhren/Tubes*, 1965-68; in the background, to the left, is Donald Baechler's *Untitled* (*Black Painting*), 1986, and to the right, Kay Rosen's *Pain*, 1997.

international art fairs, such as those in Basel, Paris, Berlin and Cologne, keep him up to date and inevitably exert a strong influence on his collection. This enables him to constantly reassess his own range of possibilities, thus generating new perspectives and focal points. Naturally, chance plays a significant role. Rather than buying conventional works, he takes bold decisions – keeping within the annual budget which he sets himself – to enrich his unusual and spectacular collection. This is where chance steps in, and he is adept at seizing opportunities: for instance, another Hamburg artist friend, Werner Büttner, was forced to sell a collection he had built up through exchanging his own works for those of friends such as Martin Kippenberger, Albert Oehlen and Georg Herold. These works now form the first of the three main pillars of the Falckenberg Collection. He supplemented this initial acquisition with pieces by major artists, often buying a whole series in a genre totally different to that of the German artists. An example of this was his discovery and acquisition of works by Americans such as Mike Kelly and Paul McCarthy, Richard Prince and John Baldessari. These form the second pillar, while the third comprises works by Dieter Roth, Vito Acconci, Franz West and Oyvind Fahlström. He became friends with the latter's widow and bought all the artist's graphic works from her. With such a rich collection, Harald Falckenberg made a powerful impression on the art world, at the same time lending active support and legitimacy to a younger generation of Postmodernists, including Eric Parker, Keith Tyson, Franz Ackermann and Thomas Hirschhorn. With others such as John Bock, Michel Majerus, Sam Durant and Jonathan Meese, these are the very young artists in his collection, which thus encompasses some of the great themes of our time – identity, globalization, power and money. It is not unusual to find these little-known artists achieving recognition in museums of contemporary art that take courage from Dr Falckenburg's bold choices; and he in turn never goes back on his decisions.

In many respects he has become the trend-setter for many curators and directors of international museums who often come to seek inspiration from his Phoenix Foundation in Hamburg-Harburg, which he created in

OPPOSITE Anteroom of the library with wall painting by Peter Kogler, *Installation*, 1998. In the background is Paul McCarthy's photographic work *Masks, Front and Side View (Pigs)*, 1998.

ABOVE Dining area of the living room with library. Between the bookcases is Juan Miguel Pozo's picture *Skat Players*, 1995.

OPPOSITE Metal sculpture *Atomic Time Guardian*, 1988, by Petrus Wandrey.

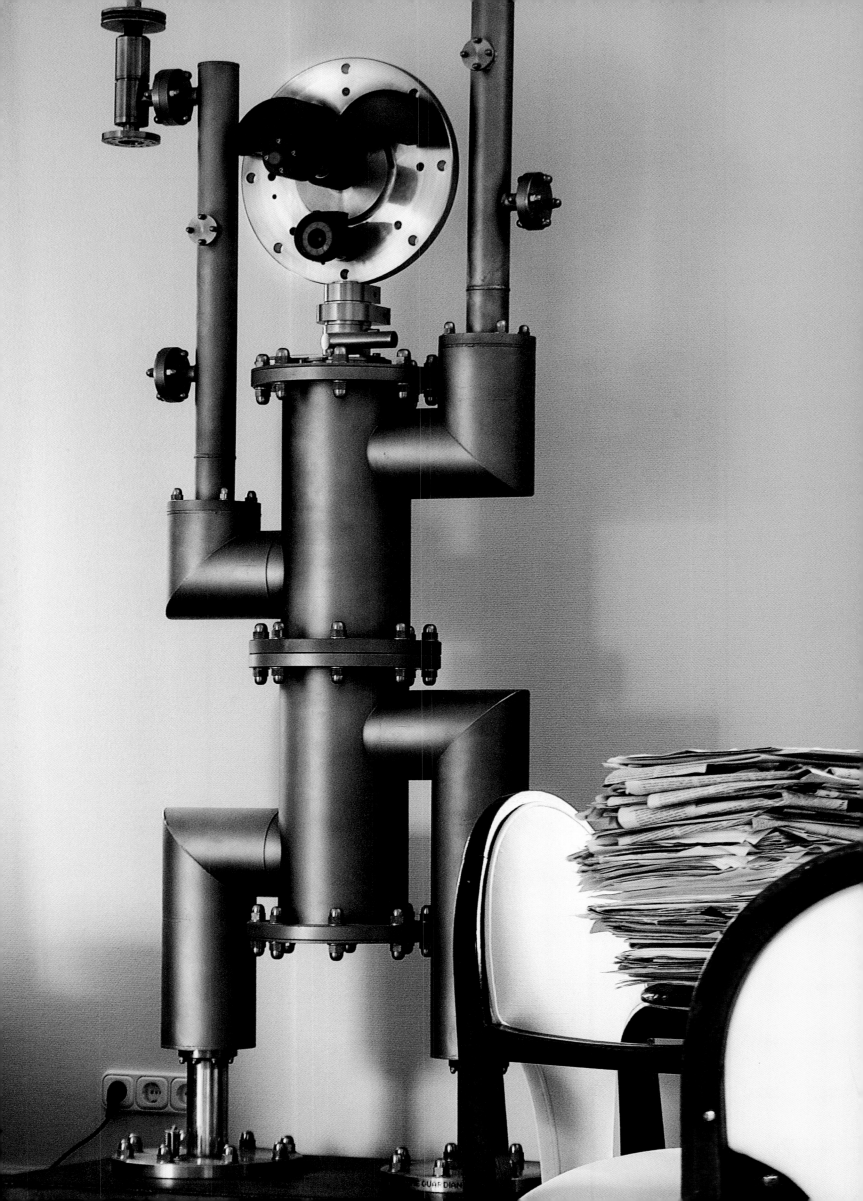

2001 in a huge, formerly industrial space, occupying some four thousand square metres. This foundation allows the public access, not only to the works in his collection, but also to those from other private collections. It also mounts thematic exhibitions devised by external organizations, generally lasting about six weeks. Harald Falckenburg is one of those exceptional collectors who has earned the attention and respect of the greatest specialists in contemporary art. The Phoenix Foundation does not have the same aspirations as traditional museums, though it commands admiration in its own right. Art students give guided tours to the public, and receive their fees in full, while entry to the foundation is free of charge for everyone.

Dr Falckenburg does not seek external advice, as he is not only confident about his own choices, but also believes in people learning from their own experiences. His passion for art is part of his daily life, which revolves around this dynamic

foundation and his private collection. He loves talking about his subject and writing books and articles, which he does very well.

As far as the future of the foundation and collection is concerned, although his children are also interested in art, he is not sure that they will want to continue this extraordinary venture, and he has devised all sorts of ideas that might extend its life meaningfully and to the benefit of all concerned. He could, for example, sell the collection later and use the profits to set up a foundation for young artists. Here is a collector who is also a true patron of the arts, as well as being a brilliant example of artistic innovation: for him, it is truly a matter of art for art's sake. One thing is certain: he will encourage many more talents to flower in the course of a rich life which has already helped many to blossom.

Erich Marx
A PATRON OF BERLIN

Chance, favourable circumstances and the ability to seize on the significance of events – these are the features that have punctuated the life of Erich Marx, a collector and patron of the arts in Berlin. Life has brought him good fortune but, in the final analysis, success always depends on what you make of your luck. This is the key to the individuality in all of us.

Erich Marx grew up in the country. The war, post-war reconstruction, and above all his own career left him very little time in which to discover art. After studying law, he worked in various publishing firms, rising rapidly in this field. Initially he was with Burda, then Hoffmann & Kampe, and finally with the daily newspaper *Hannoversche Allgemeine Zeitung*.

What fascinated him as a young man was not so much the legal aspects of publishing as the link between everyday life and economics that made the publishing world exciting.

It was quite by chance, through a project initiated by the newspaper, that he arrived in Berlin. There, after twenty years in publishing, he embarked on a second successful career, this time in property. He set up on his own, but it was around this time that he first met the associate with whom he is still working today, and with whom he would later develop a concept of real estate and *kurorte*, places where patients are sent to convalesce or for rehabilitation. He built a number of apartments and establishments – thirty-seven in all – which are still in operation today. Although he remains actively involved in the business, he is now able to devote most of his time to a passion that began in the 1970s.

It was during a holiday on the island of Sylt in the North Sea, the most northern point of Germany, that Marx first came in contact with contemporary art. He went to a small local gallery and discovered an artist whose work he liked, and so he bought five engravings. These are still to be seen today, hanging in his office. It was his first purchase of contemporary art, but not in the sense that it marked the beginning of a collection. Gradually he began to acquire more and more artworks in significant numbers and of various kinds.

LEFT Part of the Hamburger Bahnhof, the Museum of Contemporary Art in Berlin.

ABOVE RIGHT Erich Marx with an antique head.

DOUBLE PAGE OVERLEAF Interior of the Hamburger Bahnhof with works from the Marx Collection. In the background, on the left, is Anselm Kiefer's *Hoffmann von Fallersleben*, 1983/86, and to the right is his *Lilith on the Red Sea* (Lilith am Roten Meer), 1990. The installation on the floor is *Berlin Circle*, 1986, by Richard Long.

Vorsicht Stufe!

Over a period of thirty years, he lived in Berlin and met many artists, as well as getting involved in the city's contemporary art market. He was, however, self-critical, realizing that the works he was acquiring amounted to nothing more than an accumulation of pieces determined by chance and emotion, which could not be termed a collection in the proper sense of the word. The artworks, which were kept in storage, had no common feature or theme, and this became a major source of irritation to him. He needed a profile, and so he set himself the challenge of finding an idea that would link the items together, to form a real collection.

It was in 1973 that the purchase of a single work from an art gallery marked the turning point in his career as a collector. The acquisition proved to be the foundation stone of the Marx Collection, which is now internationally recognized. It was a canvas by Cy Twombly to which he felt an instinctive attraction, even though it was expensive and, as far as his friends were concerned, incomprehensible. However, chance had finally led the collector to the concept that would underlie his collection.

One day, while playing tennis with his associate,

Erich Marx told him about the picture he had purchased, and he in turn learned about a Berlin author who was writing a book about Cy Twombly. Marx's immediate reaction was, 'It would be great if my work appeared in the book.' The name of the author was Heiner Bastian. In due course they met and became firm friends, as they still are today; in fact they are neighbours. Together they discussed new focal points of interest for the collection, and it was already clear that Marx wanted to collect the international artists of his own generation. Whenever possible, he tried to acquire an ensemble of works, but it was equally important to collect those pieces that essentially illustrated the development of a leading artist. At that time, Heiner Bastian was an assistant to Joseph Beuys. He knew Andy Warhol and Robert Rauschenberg personally, was a friend of Cy Twombly, and was of course writing about this new kind of art. The works of these artists became the foundations of the Marx Collection, and many friendships were formed between this collector and the artists whom he supported.

In 1982, the Marx Collection was put on public display for the first time at the National Gallery in

Berlin. The exhibition took the art world by surprise, because until then the public had no idea that such a collection existed: all the works had previously been stored in a warehouse. On the evening of the opening, four thousand people came to see the assembled works and to meet Joseph Beuys, Andy Warhol, Robert Rauschenberg and Cy Twombly.

Another chance event was also to influence the collection. The Museum of Contemporary Art in Mönchengladbach, designed by the Viennese architect Hans Hollein, had been completed. But suddenly, a major European collector cancelled the permanent loan of his collection to the museum. Marx was delighted to seize this opportunity, by taking the other collector's place, for it meant that his works would not have to be returned to the warehouse.

The Marx Collection was exhibited for twelve years at the museum in Mönchengladbach. Meanwhile, in Berlin, it was suggested to the collector that the Hamburger Bahnhof, the old railway station for the Hamburg-Berlin line, should be converted into a museum. Marx decided to create a foundation, incorporated into what was to become the Museum of Contemporary Art, Hamburger Bahnhof. A contract was drawn up with the city, and the famous architect Josef Paul Kleihus was commissioned to renovate the station, which he did with great sensitivity, transforming it into one of the finest museums in Berlin.

In 1996, the museum which contained the Marx Collection was opened by the former Presidents of Germany, Roman Herzog and his predecessor, Richard von Weizsäcker. Today it is the permanent home for all the items from different periods that constitute the life's work of Dr Erich Marx.

In fact, the collection had already reached its climax by the opening of its exhibition in 1982, at the New National Gallery in Berlin, for it is now extremely difficult to acquire important works by the four major artists who are at the heart of the Marx Collection. Marx had achieved his personal goal, but a collector who has devoted his life to contemporary art cannot simply stop collecting, for art never ceases production. The pleasure of acquiring works and the success of the collection are the driving force that have led to its continued expansion through the work of artists such as Anselm Kiefer, Donald Judd, Keith Haring, Bruce Nauman and Günter Förg.

Erich Marx remains very close to his works. He visits the Hamburger Bahnhof regularly, and recalls the stories attached to them – the great moments that have enriched his life. Sometimes he buys more contemporary art, and he remains young at heart. Despite his international reputation and the high esteem in which he is held, both as collector and as patron of the arts, he is a modest man, with a subtle sense of humour.

RIGHT Andy Warhol's portrait of Erich Marx, 1976.

DOUBLE PAGE OVERLEAF Damien Hirst's famous sheep preserved in formaldehyde (not part of the Marx Collection).

Inge Rodenstock
THE ARTIST AS COLLECTOR

One might easily assume that Inge Rodenstock was born with a passion for art. At the age of seventeen she registered for Oskar Kokoschka's courses at the summer academy in Salzburg, but as the eldest daughter of an entrepreneur, she was expected to take over the family business. Eager instead to follow her instincts, she pursued her studies at various art schools in Düsseldorf, Munich and Paris and, without any financial support from her parents, embarked on a free and independent life. It is a choice that she has never questioned. Nor does she regret the small roles she used to play in productions by the Bavaria film studios, or the articles

she contributed to the culture pages of the weekly newspaper *Die Zeit*. She vividly recalls a number of important meetings at that time, in the mid 1960s, in particular at the Düsseldorf Academy, where she became acquainted with some of the major post-war artists, including Gerhard Richter, Gotthard Graubner and Günther Uecker. In Munich, she very soon exhibited her own work under her maiden name, Inge Haux, at the Lenbachhaus and at the home of Günther Franke.

She also became friends with the well-known gallery owner Alfred Schmela, who used to exhibit works by these young artists at the Düsseldorf Academy, as well as pieces by Joseph Beuys. She would sit in the cafés all night long discussing art with Schmela, who proved to be a wonderful mentor, taking her with him to meet artists and famous collectors such as Fänn Schniewindt who, thanks to Schmela, became the first German collector to show interest in, and indeed to buy the work of Roy Lichtenstein. This unique friendship, together with the talent and instinct of the young student, led her inevitably towards collecting, as she acquired various major works of art almost as soon as they were created. The first *Spatial Concept*, 1959, by Lucio Fontana, she bought from Schmela in 1965, paying him in monthly instalments. It was the beginning of a pursuit that has so far lasted forty years and has established her reputation as a great collector.

In the first phase of her career, her treasures ranged from paintings by Antoni Tàpies and Yves Klein, to drawings by Joseph Beuys and sculptures by Jean Tinguely, with other works by Richard Tuttle, Arman and Jannis Kounellis.

The second phase of her collecting career came about purely by chance. In 1968, she was on her first visit to New York in the company of Wolfgang Hahn, a collector and at that time a picture restorer at the Wallraf-Richartz Museum in Cologne. Visiting various American exhibitions with him, she happened to meet the great collector Peter Ludwig, who subsequently accompanied them to the galleries and studios of some of the most famous artists at that time: Roy Lichtenstein, Andy Warhol, Jasper Johns, Robert Rauschenberg and Donald Judd. It was on this trip that Peter Ludwig acquired the post-war American artworks that are now to be seen in Cologne, at the museum that bears his name. Also in New York, the young Inge bought her first Cy Twombly, for $2000, and in two weeks she had

ABOVE A Burmese head of Buddha.

OPPOSITE The drawing room, with two fabric paintings by Sigmar Polke, left and right, near the staircase; the Plexiglas lamps are an installation by Jorge Pardo.

made countless discoveries and contacts, such as the American architect and collector Philip Johnson, whose collection she saw at the museum in Connecticut.

In 1969, this delightful young woman married the Munich industrialist Rolf Rodenstock, although to begin with he was far from sharing her all-consuming passion for a form of contemporary art which the highly conservative society of Munich found extremely difficult to understand. This included certain avant-garde works of Joseph Beuys and Tom Wesselmann which had found a home with the young couple. Art does not explain itself, and sometimes needs time to be appreciated and understood. Through discussions and visits to museums, Inge's husband swiftly learned to appreciate her favourite modern artists, and he was all the more proud of her when he realized how in tune she was with developments in art. It was not long before he too was meeting artists such as Gilbert & George, and Joseph Beuys, with whom he became friends.

Inge Rodenstock had assembled and financed the collection by herself, but now she was forced to share her husband's professional duties, in his capacity as an industrialist and president of the federal union of

German industry. She frequently accompanied him on trips in Germany and abroad, and although this meant that she had less time for her collection, she was also able to benefit from such trips by visiting museums and art galleries. This helped her to gain extensive, first-hand knowledge of the international art scene. Nor did she lose her own creative instincts, which were still very strong, and during the little spare time that she had, usually at night, she illustrated seven books.

In 1972, she bought a house which she had renovated purely with the celebration of art in mind, and there she organized the very first German festival in honour of Andy Warhol, whom she had known for many years and who remained a faithful friend until his death. In parallel to the works which she had acquired as a student, Inge Rodenstock took a lively interest in Minimalist and monochrome artists such as Agnes Martin, Robert Ryman, Brice Marden, Ad Reinhardt and Hanne Darboven, all of whom were rarely to be found in German collections at that time.

It was certainly this gift for discovery that earned her a place, from 1990 to 2000, alongside other great collectors, on the board of the Solomon R. Guggenheim Museum in New York, a position which she then assumed from 2000 onwards at the Peggy Guggenheim Museum in Venice. During these years, she got to know some of the major artists of the 1980s and 1990s, who were the forerunners of contemporary art today: Jeff Koons, Mike Kelly and Cindy Sherman. She also met the 'enfant terrible' of the 1980s, Jean-Michel Basquiat, exploring New York with him and buying some of his works. Her insatiable curiosity also led her to the discovery of such British talents as Damien Hirst and Tony Cragg.

With this background, it is not surprising that the magazine *Wirtschaftswoche* asked her to write a column, giving advice on the purchase of contemporary art, for by now she was thoroughly at home in the adventurous world of 'living art'. With the same enthusiasm that had marked her activities as a student, she once again set out to travel the world, seeing things from a different perspective, renewing old friendships, and discovering new talents among collectors and artists, always on the look-out for first steps and first works,

ABOVE Private photographs in the library, including one of Joseph Beuys.

such as those of Jorge Pardo, who combines art with architecture and design.

It is a striking feature of her collection that so many of the works are by artists at the beginning of their careers. She buys them at the earliest possible opportunity, mainly from galleries, sometimes at auctions, but never directly from the artists themselves, because she recognizes and appreciates the vital role played by the gallery owner. Long experience has shown her that, while some artists are rising in profile, others are disappearing from the scene; but even if she knows that a young artist may not live up to his or her early promise, she continues to follow her intuition, based on the principle of love at first sight, and to seize any opportunity that arises.

Of course, as a collector, it is not always easy to find, let alone acquire the work one is after, and Inge knows that she must sometimes use her powers of persuasion. Such was the case with

artist Tom Sachs, from whom she bought two important works when she visited him and his gallery owner in New York. It is not so easy to say no to an experienced art lover.

Nowadays, Inge Rodenstock spends most of her time visiting international exhibitions and major art fairs, and sometimes she even draws inspiration from other collectors. She lends items from her collection to exhibitions, especially when this benefits the artists concerned. The international art world – artists, museum directors and exhibition organizers – frequently converges on the home of this generous collector, who likes nothing more than to build bridges between the different characters in this never-ending story which is the creation of art.

From the very beginning, Inge Rodenstock was an original, who followed her own path in a changing world where she could indulge her spirit of adventure. She has created a setting for her works, and maintains continuous contact with them; and although she frequently declares that she is ready to stop collecting, those who know her do not believe a word.

ABOVE The drawing room leading to the library. Above the opening is a picture by Robert Longo, *Strong in Love*, 1987; to the right is Tony Cragg's installation *Worldly Goods*, 1985.

DOUBLE PAGE OVERLEAF In the gallery is a windmill by Andreas Slominski; to the right is Ernesto Neto's sculpture *Silence in the Hole*, 1999, and on the left-hand wall is the hanging sculpture *Fruit of Thy Loins*, 1990, by Mike Kelley.

Jan and Mitsuko Shrem
ART AND WINE

Jan and Mitsuko Shrem are among that small group of exceptionally gifted people who create progress in the world by inventing new paths for themselves and for others. Coming from traditional backgrounds, they have both been outstanding in their cultures through making the most of their talents. Art is at the centre of their unique adventure together, which for Jan Shrem began with a life of travel and an instinct for taking advantage of any opportunity.

LEFT View of the vineyards in Calistoga Valley. In the foreground is the large steel sculpture *Twins*, 1972, by Richard Serra.

ABOVE Jan and Mitsuko Shrem with a mobile by Alexander Calder; in the background is Bruce Naumann's *Study for Dream Passage*, 1984.

OVERLEAF, LEFT Before the entrance to the portico, Henry Moore's bronze sculpture *Mother Earth*, 1957/58.

RIGHT The fountain entitled *Torino Royal Bacchus Brunnen*, owned by Queen Paola of Belgium: made in the 19th century from Carrara marble, the basin is finished in Cippolino marble, and the shell is made from rare golden Calacatta.

Of Lebanese origin, Jan was born in Colombia in 1930, but his family soon settled in Jerusalem where he spent his childhood. In 1946 he went to the United States to complete his studies, and in 1955 he decided to spend a two-week holiday in Japan. He ended up staying there for thirteen years, completely fascinated by a country

75

still bound to its feudal customs: this reminded him of his own youth, in an orthodox culture founded on respect for age and knowledge. It was impossible for him to find employment there, so he created his own company which quickly became hugely successful, expanding into an empire.

It was a simple but brilliant idea. He had been able to finance his studies in the United States by selling encyclopedias, in the process developing a passion for books and a firm understanding of the demand for indispensable volumes. As a result of this, he realized the potential of breaking into what he perceived to be an underdeveloped and promising field in Japan. At that time, nothing existed in the way of foreign technical and scientific writings, except old-fashioned books written in German, which had been the dominant scientific language until the Second World War. So he decided to import and thereby introduce millions of essential works written in English, and these soon became the standard reference books in these highly specialized fields. The offices which he constructed for his booming publishing business were evidence of this rapid success, reflecting his early dreams of pursuing a career in architecture.

Continuing his desire to build beautiful things, Jan Shrem also dreamed of opening a gallery of Japanese art as well as European works, which were still rare at that time in Japan. Meeting Mitsuko, who worked in his gallery, was a decisive event which sealed the precious alliance between a businessman who was already a connoisseur of ancient art, and an artist who had an instinctive eye for quality. From then on, they were always in agreement when buying art together and enjoyed a shared appreciation.

Strengthened by their early Japanese success, they sold their businesses at the end of the 1960s and left Japan to live in Europe. After a brief period in London, they settled in Milan where Jan joined the Fabbri publishing company which focused on making beautifully illustrated art books. The couple took time to travel and to visit the great European and American

ABOVE Robert Morris's aluminium *3 L-Beams*, 1965-67, with the vineyards in the background.

OPPOSITE The large drawing room with pictures (from left to right) by Poliakoff, Soulages, De Kooning, Picasso and Dubuffet. In front of the window is a marble sculpture by Hans Arp, with a painted bronze sculpture by Hans Bellmer to its right, and a metal sculpture by Takis in the background.

art exhibits such as the Venice Biennale and the Documenta in Kassel, Germany, where they familiarized themselves with the modern and contemporary artists of their generation, and began to collect their works with passion and insight.

Jan Shrem did not hesitate in travelling long distances to meet an artist in person, and would carefully examine a hundred artworks before choosing one, convinced that you cannot make a valid selection without having a properly trained eye. Instead of buying many pieces by one artist, he preferred to choose only one or just a very few, from the best period, in an attempt to avoid what he regards as the easy trap of selecting pieces through love at first sight. He wanted

artworks that would stand the test of time but, as all good collectors know, the trick is to find those pieces which, years later, continue to be interesting and to challenge the viewer.

After two years in Milan, the couple decided to leave for Paris, believing that the French city would be better suited to their children's education. They moved into a house that had been built by one of Napoleon's officials in the Parc de Montretout, belonging to the Parc de Saint Cloud district, and became friends with their neighbours, the actor Lino Ventura, and the great connoisseur and businessman Eric de Rothschild.

Frequenting artists' studios and galleries, Jan and Mitsuko Shrem wove close ties with the creative community of Paris, an approach that has given their collection uncommon range and vitality. A number of high quality artworks soon joined their first acquisition which was a Poliakoff, dating from 1940. Initially, they concentrated on Surrealists such as Salvador Dalí, Francis Picabia and Max Ernst, but they also supported the CoBrA artists Pierre Alechinsky, Karel Appel, Corneille and Constant.

ABOVE In the entrance hall and wine-tasting room hangs Jean-Paul Riopelle's *Austria III* (Autriche III), 1954.

Their collection moved on to include French artists such as Jean Dubuffet, Pierre Soulages and César, as well as the Columbian painter Fernando Botero, with whom they became friends. The pace of their collecting was intense, and they loved to attend auctions with friends to whom they were bound by a contract of loyalty: it was agreed that they would not bid against each other, but be content to draw lots in order to determine who would become the definitive owner of a particular artwork.

One of the happiest moments in Jan Shrem's life was the day that a famous Belgian collector was forced by events in his life to part with several important works in his collection, and Jan was able to acquire the most beautiful pieces.

The Shrems were not so drawn to new artists at this time, the quality of whose work it is difficult to measure over the long term; instead they preferred to wait, naturally incurring the risk of having to make a greater investment later on. There were certain exceptions, however. It was not unusual, for example, to see them actively supporting young local artists, aware of the difficulty of being recognized in a world

where talent may lead to success, but it can take a considerable time to achieve one's desired goal.

The Shrems are untiring aesthetic explorers and soon discovered, together with their friend Eric de Rothschild and several others, the extraordinary world of viticulture and wine-making. Jan Shrem began to study the subject seriously, which naturally led him to California where he and Mitsuko settled with their two sons. Beginning in the late 1970s, the state had become the new laboratory for wine-making. Today, they own vineyards in the Napa Valley, including the world-famous Clos Pegase, spending part of the year in their home which is situated on the top of a hill in the middle of their estate, the other months in San Francisco, New York and Tokyo.

Art remains at the heart of this couple's prodigious vitality and, after moving to California, they enriched their collection with new works by Minimalists such as Robert Ryman, while their vineyard resembles a magical garden filled with pieces by Dubuffet, Henry Moore, Mark di Suvero, Louise Bourgeois, Robert Morris, Richard Serra and

ABOVE In the kitchen of the private residence is a painting by Dubuffet.

Tony Cragg. These sculptures form the outdoor counterpart of the Shrems's indoor display of paintings and works on paper from the same period.

The Shrem Collection overflows with stunning artworks, representing the movements which inspired the couple: first Surrealism, then the CoBrA group, the French scene including Dubuffet and César, and Minimalism. In addition, the tasting rooms on the estate showcase a precious collection of wine vessels from Syria, the Roman Empire, China, Korea and Japan, some of which are four thousand years old. Interestingly, the Shrems had begun to explore and collect wine-making objects long before they became involved in viticulture.

In an open spirit of generosity, Jan and Mitsuko Shrem have permanently lent fifteen of their most important artworks to the San Francisco Museum of Modern Art (SFMOMA), most of which date from the Surrealist period. Working with this museum in the 1980s, they also sponsored a competition to create a winery and museum in the centre of their Clos Pegase vineyards. Architect Michael Graves was selected from a field of ninety-six entrants, and today this 'temple to wine and art' remains a highlight of any visit to northern California. The Shrems had even considered an extension to this famous museum, and Graves proposed constructing 'the grotto of Pegasus' on the top of the hill alongside the Shrems's home: the water would flow down the hill and run inside the circular museum where the artworks are on display.

Unfortunately, this daring project came up against local regulations. But it was not a serious setback, because the vineyards and museum continue to be highly popular with the public who come to tour the estate and marvel at the art. And often they can come and listen to Jan Shrem himself, who speaks with knowledge and passion, whether he is talking about Bacchus or Surrealism.

RIGHT View from the atrium of the private residence into a passage with Pierre Soulages's *3-4-55*, 1955.

DOUBLE PAGE OVERLEAF
The monumental sculpture *Spider*, 1996, by Louise Bourgeois, with a view of the Calistoga Valley.

Christoph Müller
DRAWN TO THE GOLDEN AGE

By now, Christoph Müller should long since have been given honorary citizenship of the Netherlands and Belgium. He says so himself, with a smile. As a collector who never really thought of becoming one, in just eighteen years he has amassed one of the most extensive collections in Germany, mainly from the Golden Age of 17th-century Dutch and Flemish masters.

Müller was born in Stuttgart, in 1938. His father was a journalist and publisher, and after working as an editor for the *Tagesspiegel* in Berlin, Christoph took over the family publishing firm in Tübingen in 1969. Inspired by his late friend Axel Manthey, the well-known stage designer and director, he had already begun to buy engravings in the 1960s by Andy Warhol, Roy Lichtenstein, David Hockney and other Pop artists.

One day, in his capacity as a culture editor, he went to the art fair in Munich, where a 17th-century Dutch painting called *Musical*

Company, by Anthonie Palamedesz, simply bowled him over, and he tried to find out more about the artist. He studied the painting closely, and knew that a work of this quality must be extremely valuable, to the tune of hundreds of thousands of German marks. Astonished by the very reasonable price of DM 30,000 which the dealer was asking, and carried away with enthusiasm by his discovery, he bought the painting. This work, now of international repute, was the first item in his collection. As he was later to learn, the Hermitage in St Petersburg has another, slightly different version. Initially somewhat irritated by this, he then discovered that it was not uncommon in those days for Dutch artists to paint the same subject several times. In fact there are no less than four versions of this particular painting.

Gradually, Christoph Müller formed his own personal vision of art, which grew into an unbridled passion for the great Dutch and Flemish masters. Since the Palamedesz painting was a little out of place among the Warhols and Lichtensteins, he felt that this magnificent old work was in need of company, and this was the line along which his collection subsequently

grew. He visited all the museums, not just in Holland and Belgium but all over the world, where the work of the Dutch and Flemish masters could be seen.

Initially he bought all his art from galleries, but then he began to attend the major art auctions in London, Amsterdam, Vienna and New York. Nowadays, his collection comprises one hundred and ten paintings, three hundred drawings, one thousand engravings and etchings, and about seventy emblem books – rare items which are seldom seen in German museums. These 17th-century books are identical to those used by the Dutch and Flemish artists to draw their ideas and models when they painted the 'disguised symbolism' of the Golden Age.

ABOVE *Eve from the Rib of Adam* (Eva aus dem Rippen Adams), *c.* 1600, by Raphael Coxie.

OPPOSITE The living room: on the back wall, to the left, a river landscape attributed to Jasper van der Lanen, *c.* 1600; on the shelf below, some 17th-century Dutch tiles; towards the middle on the wall, *Portrait of a Man* (Männliches Bildnis), *c.* 1650, by Moeyaert; to the right, *Cave* (Höhle), by Rombout van Troyen, painted in the first half of the 17th century.

Müller developed his collection along two very distinct lines: the Dutch line of Rembrandt, influencing the north, and the Flemish line of Rubens, who left his indelible mark on the south. From these different worlds he collected everything, beginning with three 15th-century engravings of Burgundy, and including genre paintings, seascapes, landscapes, still lifes, right through to the 'vanitas' paintings of the late 17th century. The architectural paintings of Steenwyck, Neefs, van Vliet and Nickel formed another important focal point.

When it came to portraits, however, he took his time, for nothing reveals a collector's character so much as his choice of portraits. As Müller himself says, identification with a portrait is essential for a collector, and so far he has only ten. His collection has been shown at many exhibitions, the largest in Tübingen in 2004, and has also been published in f our catalogues. He is always happy to lend his works to major exhibitions, for instance to one in Graz in 2003, which focused on European art.

With all his expertise, Christoph Müller loves to show off these works at different exhibitions, and has even gone so far as to conduct guided tours that last four hours and certainly beat all records when it comes to time, learning and sheer enthusiasm. In the circumstances, it is not surprising that he often receives

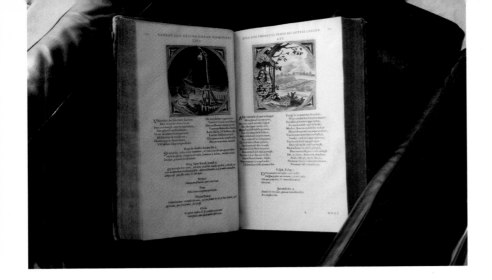

letters from those who have listened to him, thanking him for these unforgettable talks. He finds this all the more touching as he himself feels that a collector is deeply indebted to the work itself and to the vision of the artist who created it.

It was in this spirit that Christoph Müller set up a foundation in 1999 to merge his own magnificent collection of engravings with that of Berlin. Today, the head of the department of Dutch copper engravings in Berlin chooses works which he considers to be important and which have come up for sale on the market, and Christoph Müller buys them – on condition, of course, that he also likes them.

The most important item in the Müller Collection is an oil painting by Simon de Vlieger, *Shipwreck off a Rocky Coast*, which he acquired from the famous Czernin Collection. He also has drawings and engravings by this influential artist, who was well known for his marine subjects, among others. Vlieger's precursor, Jan Pocellis, and his successor, Wilhelm van de Velde, also play an integral part in a collection that has gradually been accumulated over the years.

Thanks to his extensive studies, a very powerful and personal bond has developed with the Dutch world, basically *his* world, although he is soon to take up residence in Berlin, for that is where most of his collection has, as it were, migrated. Wherever his works go, he goes too. So far, every item has been transported back to his Bauhaus-style home in Tübingen, but now he is going to retire and is excited at the prospect of living right in the heart of the German art world, amid the contemporary galleries of Berlin. He says, 'Even the most recent art has both direct and indirect links to the work of the Old Masters, but only someone who knows modern art can perhaps understand the thinking of those Old Masters.'

ABOVE First edition of a very rare emblem book by Jacob Cats, 1625. It is open at *Preparations for a Wedding* (Hovwelyck).

OPPOSITE Bedroom, with (above) seascapes by Aert Anthonisz and Pieter Mulier the Elder and (below) Ludolf Backhuysen and Jan Porcelis. In the top row of paintings, above the head of the bed, are interiors by Pieter Willemsz, Van der Stock, Hendrick Cornelisz van Vliet and Isaak van Nickele. In the bottom row, *View of a Gothic Church at Night* (Blick in eine gotische Kirche bei Nacht), *c.* 1630, by Peeter Neefs the Elder, and *Evening Service in a Gothic Church* (Abendlicher Gottesdienst in einer gotichen Kirche), *c.* 1590, by Hendrick van Steenwyck the Elder.

Lieselotte and Ernest Tansey
THE JOURNEY OF THE MINIATURES

Lieselotte and Ernest Tansey have greatly enriched the region in which they live, thanks to their generous foundation and collection of miniatures. Lieselotte has brought about a major expansion of Celle, near Hanover in Germany, as the heiress to an oil dynasty: her father was himself the son of an oil pioneer who, at the age of eighteen, had gone to Sumatra as a prospector, before setting up a company in 1914 which spread worldwide after the First World War.

Lieselotte initially studied in Heidelberg and Berlin, before going to New York for a short time in 1938, where she stayed with friends of her father. Straight away, she loved America. When she returned home, her father sent her first to Vienna and then to Berlin to gain experience, after which she started work in Celle as a secretary at the headquarters of her father's firm.

The family lost the entire business during the Second World War, but a few years later were fortunate enough to regain some of their possessions. In 1957, while working for the company again, Lieselotte met an American named Ernest Tansey, and married him a year later. In 1969, the couple left the business in order to travel, especially around Asia and North and South America: they brought back a lot of art, often large works that were difficult to transport. So one day, as this elegant lady recounts, at the beginning of the 1970s, they decided to concentrate on miniatures, pictures that vary from small to tiny. This decision was certainly inspired by the three miniatures that she had inherited from her mother, although at the time no one had dreamed that these might mark the beginning of an exceptional collection that would be known all over the world.

Lieselotte Tansey's increasing expertise and keen eye impressed a London dealer who had once been based in Celle as an army officer, and he became the first of many specialist accomplices in the search for beautiful objects. These were to be found all over Europe, yet it is well known that the cradle of the miniature lies in England.

The first miniatures date from the end of the Middle Ages through the beginning of the Renaissance, and were sometimes used as decorative features on boxes or jewelry, though they were mainly worn as pendants or

LEFT In the living room is an 18th-century oval still life with flowers by Gérard van Spaendonck, and in front of this painting are two French marble amphorae, decorated with gilded brass, c. 1800.

93

displayed on walls. By its very nature and intimate scale, the miniature was a personal object which people liked to keep close to them – perhaps the portrait of a loved one – but at the same time it had a symbolic function, given as an honour, a betrothal offering, or a diplomatic gift. The miniature was originally the exclusive reserve of the aristocracy, who in certain stately homes had cabinets full of such paintings: galleries of ancestors, landscapes and genre scenes.

Later, in the 18th and early 19th centuries, the middle classes discovered these little gems which could be painted to order. The genre was also influenced in the second half of the 18th century by the discovery of ivory, which became a favourite material for the artists. This period is superbly represented in the Tanseys's collection, although they have many rare works that extend over four centuries and cover all kinds of subject matter: portraits, still lifes and the more unusual landscapes. It was not until the end of the 19th century that the fashion for miniatures began to fade away, in the light of the increasingly popular art of photography.

ABOVE LEFT Casket with miniature portraits from the Tansey Collection.

ABOVE RIGHT Miniature by Anton Friedrich König, c. 1760, probably depicting Prince Heinrich of Prussia and his wife.

94

The oldest miniatures in the collection date from the 16th century, including portraits of Ludwig Landgraf of Hesse and his wife Maria Markgräfin of Brandenburg-Kulmbach, painted in 1585, while the most recent works are by artists in the early 20th century. One finds the names of many famous artists: Augustin, Isabey, Périn, Lemoine, Sicardi and Weiler from France; Smart, Cosway, Meyer and Engleheart from England; Rosalba Carriera, the best known of all the Italian miniature painters; the Austrians Füger and Daffinger, and artists from Scandinavia and Germany. Most of these miniatures have been bought at auctions, but some have come from private collections, as the result of long and patient work by the couple, and there has been a continual refinement of taste and attention to detail, all of which has given rise to a collection that fills two catalogues.

In 1997 the Tanseys, who have no children, gave a large part of their collection to an independent foundation which is now based at the Bomann Museum in Celle – one of the most important museums of cultural history in northern Germany.

Here, next to an exhibition hall where items from the collection are displayed thematically, is a study centre which is equipped for specialist research and houses a rich library of literature on miniature painting. There is also a team of experts, including a curator, restorer and photographer, whom the couple appointed to look after the collection and to draw up a complete and informative inventory.

In the meantime, other national and international museums have shown, and continue to show great interest in this passion for miniatures, and the Tansey Collection has travelled to Brussels, Geneva and Milan. It is also permanently open to the public in Celle. Here too, the pleasure of sharing their passion ensures that the couple maintain a lust for life and remain active and thoroughly committed.

This, however, is not the end of the collectors' story. In addition to the miniatures, there are a number of paintings by some of the great masters, from Gérard van Spaendonck to Peter Bout, a pupil of Philips Wouwerman, and Hubert Drouais. The Tanseys also have a large collection of Celle silverware from the 18th and 19th centuries which is comparable to the highly prestigious silverware of Augsburg. They have amply demonstrated their talents as collectors, but they are also generous sponsors and have financed medical research into breast cancer in the United States, where a new institute in New Orleans has been named after its founder, Lieselotte Tansey.

The couple's fascination with art and their commitment to society do not simply reflect a personal sense of duty, for these things in turn enrich their own lives, constantly offering them new perspectives and projects, as well as bringing contacts and friends from all over the world. Their chief delight, however, is that together they have helped to inspire a lasting and widespread interest in the art of the miniature.

ABOVE Miniature portraits, (left) *Hébert de Stacpool*, 1853, by Louis Henri de Fontenay, and (right) *Lady in a Black Dress in front of a Red Curtain* (Dame in schwarzem Kleid vor rotem Vorhang), 1852, by Cécile Villeneuve née Colombert.

ABOVE The living room. In the centre, on the far wall, is a small landscape with a white horse painted by Philips Wouwerman; to the left, *Painting with Lake and Mountain Landscape* (Gemälde mit See und Berglandschaft), by the Flemish artist Pieter Bout, a pupil of Wouwerman, both 17th century. On the right is a baroque cupboard with ivory intarsia.

OPPOSITE Also in the living room is this portrait of Madame de Pompadour, *c.* 1756, by Hubert Douais.

Pieter C. W. M. Dreesmann
THE STORY BEHIND THE ART

A distinguished art lover, Pieter Dreesmann was brought up in a well-known collector's family in Amsterdam. His father, Dr Anton C. R. Dreesmann, was not only a remarkable businessman but also professor of economics at the University of Amsterdam. Famous for his eclectic collection of French furniture and Old Master paintings and drawings, he was also fascinated by *objets d'art* and Dutch silver. Growing up in this environment, surrounded by art, Pieter had the opportunity to study the art of being a connoisseur for thirty-five years before becoming a collector himself.

After completing his economics studies in Amsterdam, Pieter began his career with the Heineken brewery company in Holland, first in management and sales, then later in a general management position in their distilling division in Nigeria. After several years with Heineken, he worked on a temporary basis in the family business, before moving to a real estate firm in Belgium. He then began to develop the idea of forming his own company.

Of the five children in his family, Pieter was the only one to accompany his father to the antique fairs and art galleries of Delft, Maastricht, London and New York. Slowly he familiarized himself with the world of connoisseurs, becoming acquainted with the many manoeuvres necessary to enter into the field of collecting Old Master paintings. The very first artwork he acquired was an 18th-century French *tric-trac* (backgammon) table by Jacques Dubois, which he bought from a gallery in Paris. Reading books in his father's library, he had become knowledgeable about this period and the particular style of 18th-century craftsmanship.

A passionate collector, Pieter is an equally erudite researcher whose interests lie in the relationship between art and history. He is always wanting to understand the story behind each work of art. Much study and effort are required to achieve the level of expertise needed to collect Old Masters and to fully appreciate them: the market for such works is not as transparent as it is for the arts of later periods.

Cabinet paintings on panel by 17th-century Dutch painters form the principal part of his collection. With

99

exceptional pieces by Hendrick Avercamp, Salomon van Ruysdael, Willem Claesz Heda, Willem van de Velde the Younger and Adriaen Coorte, these marine paintings, portraits, still lifes and landscapes from the dawn of the Golden Age of painting in Holland quite naturally hold pride of place among all his artworks.

Half a century before Holland achieved formal independence from Spain, in 1648, it chartered the Vereenigde Oostindische Compagnie (the VOC or East India Trade Company), and there followed an era of great geographic and aesthetic exploration, so admired by Dreesmann. Established in Amsterdam in 1602, the VOC was the first truly multinational company in the world, and the voyages that it organized and financed to places such as Australia, the West Indies, Southeast Asia. made international trade and consequently economic power possible for the tiny country of Holland.

History demonstrates that art and creativity are strongly linked to a community's increased wealth. The rise of patronage in Holland grew rapidly because of the new economic conditions and it generated an explosion of imagination and new forms of expression in the world of painting and the decorative arts. Art historians believe that perhaps up to a million paintings were produced in Holland during its golden years in the 17th century.

The historical context of artworks enthrals Dreesmann who, before acquiring a work of art, conscientiously studies the period in which it was created. When he bought his first 17th-century Old Master painting at the TEFAF Maastricht art fair ten years ago, he considered many paintings by the same artist before deciding on one. This still life painting by Balthasar van der Ast hangs today in his kitchen, where he can enjoy his first acquisition on a daily basis.

Dreesmann's focus on 17th-century Dutch Old Masters is linked, no doubt, to his education and upbringing, but his taste for works on paper by Pablo Picasso certainly derives from a personal fascination with the artist. His collection is built on two different approaches: firstly, he loves to surround himself with

ABOVE A Chinese death mask from the Liao dynasty, AD 907-1124, in the library.

OPPOSITE The large drawing room. On the left wall, *The Dancer Sada Yacco* (La Danseuse Sada Yacco), 1900/01, by Pablo Picasso. On the table is the bronze *Grand Arabesque, in three-four time* (Grande Arabesque, troisième temps), *c.* 1919/1921, by Edgar Degas; and behind is Picasso's *Head of a Madman* (Tête de Fou), before 1939.

key works by different masters from one clearly defined period, secondly to collect significant pieces by one artist that represent his or her various styles.

His collecting approach was more spontaneous when he bought his first watercolour by Picasso – a study for *The Absinthe Drinker* (La Buveuse d'Absinthe), dated 1901. He had, of course, read much about Picasso's life and work, but the decision to acquire the piece was made very quickly, in the space of half an hour, while visiting a gallery during a short stay in Paris twelve years ago. He spotted the watercolour from Picasso's Blue period and was immediately drawn to it. The gallery owner began to explain the background of the work, but told the young collector that it was, regrettably, not for sale. However, this statement only served to excite his interest even further. Dreesmann convinced the dealer to sell the work, and asked him to step away for five minutes to think about the lowest price he would consider selling it for. The collector made it clear that there would be no further negotiations and that he would simply say yes or no to the figure. In three minutes the gallery owner returned and the deal was done. Today this work hangs in Dreesmanns collection alongside other precious drawings, watercolours and pastels by Picasso, and he has never regretted this instinctive decision, based on love at first sight. Picasso's works on paper are among his favourites because, to his mind, drawings reflect the artist's true eye: 'A drawing catches the artist in the eyes,' he says. An oil painting can be altered many times, changes being seldom apparent, but modifications to a drawing are always visible.

It can be difficult and can take a long time to find an artwork with enough character for his collection, but Pieter Dreesmann is not the sort of man who lets a work that he loves just slip away. Whenever possible, he likes to hang the painting or drawing under consideration on his walls for several days or even weeks, to determine whether the piece is right for him. This is understandable, for his intention is to look at the artwork for the next thirty years. He wants to live with his collection and, so far, has never had second thoughts about any of his acquisitions.

LEFT Above the fireplace in the large drawing room is J. Neil Rodgers's painting *A brahma hen standing on a plinth*, 2003. The room is lit by a Louis XV chandelier, *c.* 1750.

ABOVE RIGHT *Still Life with Silver Cup, Clock and Tin Plate* (Stilleben mit Silber-Becher, Uhr und Zinnteller), 1633, by Willem Claesz Heda.

The books on the shelf are labelled: Der Nautiluspokal by Hanns-Ulrich Mette, ARENT DE GELDER by J.W. VON MOLTKE, SOUTINE I, and SOUTINE II.

When he moved into his elegant London apartment, he told his Belgian interior designer to provide enough walls for his art as well as for his books, another one of his passions. With exquisite taste and a love of detail, he has decorated his charming library with many fine *objets d'art* such as a nautilus shell cup encrusted in ivory and silver from the Augsburg period, around 1680, and a Chinese copper death mask from the Liao dynasty (AD 907-1124). On another shelf, one can find pre-Columbian sculptures from the Valdivia culture, a people who lived in Ecuador (3500-1800 BC) and even a crocodile skull from the Nile. The entire library reflects the lively, humorous and inquisitive qualities of a collector who loves to explore and who discovers as much through the beautifully illustrated books as through the works which retrace the history of art. In fact every painting,

ABOVE The skull of a Nile crocodile resting on a book in the library.

drawing and *objet d'art* is connected to another work of art or to a book in his collection. He was, for example, delighted to find a photograph by Dora Maar of Picasso, who was in the process of drawing her portrait on 17th August 1937. That very portrait now also hangs on the collector's walls. Or sometimes he tries to reconstruct still life paintings by gathering together authentic objects from the period in which the painting was created.

His profound interest in research and his curiosity about the background of each work of art is perfectly suited to the firm which he founded six years ago. His father had once asked him to find a company or individual who would be able to register the family's collection electronically in a clear, informative and precise manner. No such service existed, so Dreesmann created The Art Document Company, based in The Hague, The Netherlands, which specializes in archiving

collections, whether private or public, and researching data on all types of artworks. His experience as a collector and his connoisseurship have served to build a research centre, which helps to preserve art and its history for future generations.

A modern Maecenas, Pieter Dreesmann continues in the great tradition of art patronage, both in a professional and personal sense. His collection stands for excellence, and the dedication he has shown to his passion for art has created a collector of enormous culture and taste, who loves not only the artwork itself but also the history which gives it true meaning.

ABOVE In the passage, opposite the library, *Dora with a Chignon* (Dora au Chignon), 1937, by Pablo Picasso; on the table below is Kees Verkade's bronze, *Dr Anton C. R. Dreesmann*, 1998.

DOUBLE PAGE OVERLEAF The large drawing room. To the left of the window are two still lifes by Adriaen Coorte; to the right is *Sailing Ship and Other Small Boats on a River* (Segelschiff und andere kleine Boote auf einem Fluss), *c.* 1650, by Salomon Jacobsz van Ruysdael.

Gilles Fuchs
THE BEGINNINGS OF ART

Gilles Fuchs has the soul of a young man. He loves beginnings, young talents, the gallery owners who support them, and anyone who commits himself or herself to art that has not yet achieved recognition. Although he is particularly concerned with promoting young artists who live in France, his collection is very open and reveals a sense of humour which can no doubt be traced back to his English lineage, via his mother, and an Oxford education that instilled in him an intense dislike of earnestness and ostentation.

Fuchs was born in Paris, his father the director of the Fragonard perfumery in Grasse. Following the family tradition, he studied law in France and England, even taking a doctorate. In 1958 he married Marie-Françoise Ricci, who has remained his companion ever since and herself leads a very active life, pursuing a career in medicine. Gilles Fuchs entered the firm of Nina Ricci at the invitation of his father-in-law, who put him in charge of exports for this prestigious brand; and for thirty years he made a great success of the job. In 1988, he took over as head of the company after the death of its president.

In parallel to his professional career, Fuchs developed a true passion for art, which he regards above all as a matter of character and culture. His father, a man of great curiosity and a certain eccentricity, had shown him the way by collecting ceramics from the Middle East, and initially this was the line that he too followed, collecting earthenware together with Asiatic and pre-Columbian pottery. If you ask him at what age he began, he will burst out laughing, telling you that he already had all his teeth!

When he was about thirty, he turned his attention to contemporary art, inspired by a family friend named René de Montaigu, who was an assiduous collector and at the time had one of the finest modern collections. It was extremely varied, and fascinated the young man, particularly the American works – including Pop Art – which were not so common in French collections in the early 1960s, and also some pieces by French artists, about whom René would talk with great passion. Through this mentor, Gilles Fuchs gradually became acquainted with all the artists of the period, whom

LEFT The drawing room. Standing between the windows is a work by Bernard Pagès, *Cyprus Column* (Colonne en cyprès), 1980, beside a painting by Sicilia, *Tulip with Black Band* (Tulipe avec bande noire), 1985-87. To the right is Perramant's *Catwoman*, 2000.

ABOVE Gilles Fuchs.side

109

René de Montaigu invited to his home, just as his disciple would constantly do in later years. That, says Gilles, is how he 'got hooked'. Living in the south of France, René was in close contact with the artists of the School of Nice, not particularly well known but very charming – artists such as Armand, Roualdes, Gillie and Martial Raysse.

It occurred to Fuchs that Arman could make him a collection of Nini Ricci perfume bottles, and he persuaded René to overcome his reservations. This first commission was all the more encouraging because he was immensely enthusiastic about Arman's designs. He also remembers vividly the first time he visited Raymond Hains, who at the time was living in a cramped hotel bedroom near the Sorbonne in Paris: the meeting was inevitably very intimate and in a sense quite moving. Gilles bought some of his torn posters, political posters and metal plates, surprising himself by doing so. He remembers: 'I still didn't know anything about contemporary art, and I knew nothing at all about the Nouveau Réalistes, their daring approach and the intellectual context in which it all took place, but I was curious about it and I had something like…a kind of instinctive urge. I must say that when I got home with those metal plates and posters, I remember I put them in a room that I didn't use, and I went and had a look at them, feeling a bit worried and asking myself, "But what on earth is it?" And I didn't have a clue!'

Nothing has changed. He is still just as amazed by his choices, as if somehow his personality becomes split in two before the magical powers of these mysterious works which impose their charms and invite him to reflect. For the collector, being confronted with them is mainly a matter of sensation, a communion with the spirit – all the more effective because he feels somewhat 'violated' and shocked. If Gilles Fuchs is a hedonist, and if collecting is first and foremost an almost sensual act for him, nevertheless the 'spirit' soon manages to express itself: he is well known for his gift for words when talking about art, for while he loves to discover it, he also loves to help others discover it too.

He still believes, however, that contact with the works themselves is more important than anything you

LEFT View of the Sacré Coeur from the office window. Outside the window is a glass ball installation by Brigitte Nahon.

ABOVE RIGHT Huang Yong Ping's sculpture *Spiderweb*, 1997.

111

can say about them, and you must live with them because they can change your view of the world and transform you inwardly. They occupy as much space in your life, he says, as human beings, because they speak to you and they have an immensely strong presence.

His wife Marie-Françoise follows him discreetly through this adventure, always watching with close attention, even though she does not accompany him when he visits artists' studios. Their intellectual exchanges are ongoing, based on affectionate understanding and humour, and it is a delight to see them enjoying art together.

Ever since he began collecting, following the example of his mentor René de Montaigu, Gilles Fuchs has demonstrated a broad-minded approach and curiosity, utterly devoid of any sectarianism, leading him to embrace the School of Nice, but also artists such as Jean-Pierre Raynaud and Christian Boltanski, as well as Jean-Michel Meurice and Jean Le Gac, both of whom

LEFT Gilles Fuchs's office. Above the spiral staircase is a photograph entitled *Faceless*, 1994, by Shirin Neshat. On the left, beside the staircase, is an untitled painting by Viallat.

ABOVE RIGHT The shadow of the rabbit becomes the silhouette of Joseph Beuys on the wall: *Metamorphosis* by Markus Raetz.

have become personal friends.

Over the years, his taste has certainly evolved, but he has remained faithful to youth and to that moment when no one can be sure what will become of a work. Such choices are inevitably risky and sometimes he has to admit to mistakes. He believes that he has made some, but everything is relative: even if the works he has acquired are not all of the same high quality, he is not a man to harbour regrets and has a soft spot for every one of them. When he talks about famous artists, he likes to quote a line from Théodore de Banville: 'Posterity whose horizon is constantly shifting.' The most important thing for Gilles Fuchs is that one should be true to oneself, for it is essential that the artworks you acquire will always remain in contact with you, in one way or another.

Missing out on an important artist is therefore one of the collector's potential 'mistakes', but this does not concern him because he has not set out to assemble an historical collection. His main purpose is pleasure. He would not want to institutionalize his works by establishing a foundation or museum, because at heart he does not even regard himself as a professional

113

ABOVE Christian Boltanski's installation *Showcase of Reconstruction* (Vitrine de Reconstitution), 1972.

collector, and he does not want to be categorized in any way by the art world. His passion is not a cult, and he does not seek to create an 'oeuvre', for as he says of the works with an explosive laugh, 'It's the artists who make them.' He defines himself simply as 'an honest man' in the 18th-century sense of the term, and for him collecting is simply a nice way of helping him 'to get through life – that's all.'

Gilles Fuchs is well aware of how much he owes to all these artists, for he has received so much from them and feels that he could never give as much in return. His activity as a patron is therefore founded on a spirit of thoughtful beneficence, which he has sought to expand by setting up an association in 1994, ADIAF, to help and support artists in France. Thanks to him, about one hundred and fifty collectors pooled their experience and knowledge in order to evaluate the contemporary art scene in France and to give it the international profile which had been sadly lacking. Just as the German Expressionists and the Viennese School were ignored in France after the war, contemporary French artists who are not part of the mainstream are also completely unknown, even in their home country. The purpose of ADIAF is therefore to promote such art and to enrich the current art scene by organizing touring exhibitions abroad and awarding an annual Marcel Duchamp Prize to a particularly original young artist living in France, whose work will then be exhibited at the Musée National d'Art Moderne.

In this context, ADIAF also approaches French companies, or firms that are active in France, and invites them to participate in contemporary art by becoming patrons, thus helping to spread French culture abroad. For Gilles Fuchs, its president, artists are the finest ambassadors for a country and its culture: Matisse 'sells' France just as well as TGV, and Rothko is a better advertisement for America than Coca-Cola. Art presents the brightest credentials of a living, dynamic country and, to the collector's mind, the spiritual spice of life on an international scale comes from artists and

thinkers, not from politicians. When he was running Nina Ricci, he himself acted as an art patron by financing exhibitions, allowing artists such as Daniel Buren to showcase their works in his shop windows, and by getting Sol LeWitt to design packaging for his perfumes and cosmetics.

Gilles Fuchs sees clearly, however, that it is difficult to always remain in such close contact with contemporary art. He knows that art is anything but routine, and the fact that one might have been looking at it for fifty years does not mean that one sees any more than an art lover who has only been looking at it for ten years. He regards art as a state of mind, an openness, but also as a means of maturing; he feels that he has changed in his approach to artworks over the years, and understands them more profoundly, is better at analysing them, and sees things now that he did not necessarily see before. He no longer needs to be shocked into paying attention. From the immediate impact he has now moved to a more searching reflection on what it is that inspires an artist to create.

Gilles Fuchs's apartment is much like the man himself: very original, and subtly elegant. It has a magnificent view of the Seine and the Louvre, while the furniture and artworks give the impression not of luxury but of individuality, the entrance for example being in the form of a black and white dining room designed by Daniel Buren. Any art lover will be delighted by the changing rhythms of the layout: a large 'continent' by Hirschhorn (who was awarded the Marcel Duchamp Prize), little coloured characters by Fabien Verschaere which are spread out over a table and are no doubt being watched by the fish in Pierrick Sorin's aquarium, to the accompaniment of insistent music; whilst mingling with the fauna at the bottom is the dancing silhouette of the artist. The shadow projected onto the wall is from Markus Raetz's sculpture *Rabbit Hat*, reflecting the image of Joseph Beuys and cutting through the irony of a painting by

ABOVE The living room is dominated by Carole Benzaken's painting *Brea night Los Angeles*, 2002. To the left, beside the window, is Gaston Chaissac's striking *Totem*, 1958.

115

the young artist Carole Benzaken, who won the Marcel Duchamp Prize in 2004; while the fireplace is decorated by some Alan McCollum vases. Fuchs will also introduce you to Chinese artists who attracted his attention many years ago – he supported Chen Zhen, Wang Du and Ming very early in their careers – as well as some young Russians, whose strange works he recently acquired and are unlike anything to be seen in the current art world. There is also Adam Adach's 'red cross', and the subtly erotic photographs of the Japanese artist Noritoshi Mirakawa, nonchalantly standing on the floor of the collector's office, in stark contrast to Brigitte Nahon's 'crystal balls' which decorate one of the windows overlooking the roof of the Louvre. The office also houses one of Shirin Neshat's 'veiled women', some pieces by Tremblay, a photograph of licentious scenes from Japan by Nan Goldin, and a mural by Rutault.

In his *pensoir*, where the ballet dancer Nureyev once had his lodgings, Fuchs keeps the most provocative and often most erotic of his works.

He does not quite know why, and perhaps one should not expect any logical explanation. He will convey his message simply with a humorous comment and a screwing up of those laughing brown eyes.

ABOVE The fireplace.

OPPOSITE Francesco Clemente's painting *Inner room*, 1983, beside the entrance to the dining room.

116

Pierre Bergé
A PASSION SHARED

It is difficult and perhaps even presumptuous to assess the achievements of a man such as Pierre Bergé. He arrived in Paris at the age of eighteen, not wishing to study because he did not want to enter into any system, but he was to become one of the most brilliant French businessmen, joining forces with Yves Saint Laurent to found the famous fashion house. Together they also assembled a collection of books, paintings, sculptures, furniture and *objets d'art* that is quite exceptional. They have now set up a foundation devoted to fashion and art, in which their passions can flourish and at the same time benefit the public, whom they invite to share their pleasure.

Pierre Bergé is a man committed to many causes. He demands the highest standards, and speaks his mind loud and clear – even at the risk of alienating and shocking people, which doesn't concern him at all. In the course of his life, he has become involved in more and more fields and has occupied prestigious posts in numerous organizations: fashion, the theatre, music and social work. To list only the most well known,

LEFT The fireplace, decorated with a large mirror.

ABOVE A love of detail: the handle of the magnifying glass is made from ivory.

he co-founded and ran the Yves Saint Laurent fashion house, was president of the Opéra National de Paris, initiated the building of the Opéra Bastille, and recently opened an auction house. He is heavily involved in the organization SOS Racisme, is president of the action group against Aids, also a goodwill ambassador for UNESCO, and was instrumental in founding the gay magazine *Têtu*. He is a member of many boards and committees, and is a charismatic personality. How does he juggle all these different activities? 'First of all,' he replies, 'I don't know if I do juggle them! But at the moment I haven't dropped too many of the balls – fortunately! As I am completely agnostic and don't believe in a second life at all, we have to do as many things as we can in the only life that we have!'

When you meet Pierre Bergé, your first impression is of a man who is rather dry and unapproachable, but then he rapidly engages you in conversation, revealing a personality that is full of enthusiasm and charm, with a lively expression and a constant air of calm control. He can handle the humorous as well as the serious, and behind the sometimes stinging remarks there is a good

119

deal of tenderness. For a man who does not set out to be liked, he has won over many a celebrity. Even when he was young, he became friends with the writer Jean Giono, in whose home he lived for a while, and then with Jean Cocteau, becoming his literary executor. François Mitterand was another close friend.

Despite his contacts with such major figures, he nevertheless claims that he is no socialite, and when you ask him if he leads a bourgeois existence, he replies indignantly, 'Definitely not!' He is not interested in dining out, and if he is sometimes seen with certain big-name celebrities, it is because they have been friends for forty years and not because they are good for his image.

Music was his first passion, and even when he was young he was already familiar with the artistic world, having played the violin since childhood. He came to literature a little later, and on the island of Oléron, where he was born, he dreamed of becoming a journalist or writer. Once he arrived in Paris, his first job was with a bookshop, buying and reselling first and rare editions, and this brought him into contact with the world of collectors. He also started up a radical literary magazine.

His passion for books gave rise to a collection which now numbers more than three thousand volumes, divided between a reference section on art and an exceptional number of first editions. These include Montaigne's *Essais* (1580), Louise Labé (1515), Pascal's *Pensées*, and *Madame Bovary* and *La Tentation de Saint Antoine* by Flaubert, who is without doubt his favourite author and, in his eyes, by far the greatest of them all. What he loves almost sensually about these first editions is the fact that the books were once handled by readers of that period, and sometimes by readers who were famous in their own right: for instance, his copy of *Madame Bovary* once belonged to none other than Victor Hugo.

OPPOSITE The drawing room, with scenes from a ballet by Roland Petit starring Zizi Jeanmaire at the Casino de Paris in 1972.

DOUBLE PAGE OVERLEAF On the wall are four portraits of Yves Saint Laurent by Andy Warhol, 1972; and in front is a video about the designer's life. To the right are three display dummies wearing 'African dress', 1967. Their hair is made of human hair with wooden beads, and they are wearing the first plastic jewelry ever to have been used in haute couture.

As for paintings, he was nineteen when he met the artist Bernard Buffet, and for eight years followed his career assiduously. Initially, just after the Second World War, Buffet's powers of expression were exceptional, but then he lost his way in repetition, 'becoming literary in his plastic creations' and forgetting 'true painting', Bergé regrets, 'at the very moment when painters in the United States were finding the real sense of painting by renouncing all types of image. He didn't understand this.' Nevertheless, it was thanks to Bernard Buffet that Pierre Bergé discovered the world of art and developed his own 'intimate relationship' with it. Even though Buffet had neither taste for, nor understanding of contemporary art, he did pass on his obsession for 'great painting', and together they discovered the artists who would remain for ever in Bergé's personal pantheon: David, Delacroix, Géricault, Chassériau, Ingres – that 'absolutely admirable' 19th-century Frenchman – Poussin, and the Italian Renaissance painter Paolo Uccello. After a trip to Italy, Giotto and Piero della Francesca also joined this list of artists. The

discovery of painting brought about a radical change in Pierre Bergé's life, although even today he still writes his books and regards music and theatre as his indispensable passions. But often it was in museums that he would find peace and quiet, enabling him to recharge his batteries during key moments in his life, sometimes moments of great difficulty. He says that he would never dream of 'going on holiday to a place where there isn't at least one museum, and if there happens to be an opera house as well, so much the better…then it's a real holiday! Just to go to the seaside or the mountains would bore me stiff!'

Bergé shares his collection with Yves Saint Laurent, and they have always bought things together, agreeing even when they have chosen separately, with no problem of accountability, even though they maintain their individual tastes and independence. With this combined love of art, they have assembled their collection with great discernment. Bergé demands quality, relevance and originality, and this is amply demonstrated in the collection, which depends on no

121

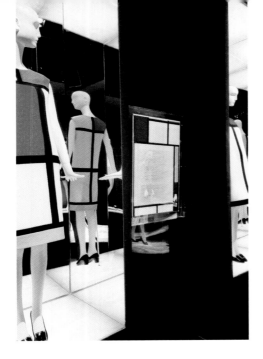

chronological order or any other extraneous influence.

For his part, Bergé has assembled the collection in accordance with personal taste, which he regards as the ultimate criterion, even if that may seem shocking to some: 'Picasso before Cubism is of little interest to me,' he freely admits, 'and afterwards is of no more interest either, apart from a few exceptions.' He has acquired works from Picasso's Cubist period, of which he is particularly fond, and he is very responsive to the years 1913-14, which was a time of profound artistic originality for Picasso. His work by Giacomo Balla also dates from 1914. He is very reticent about his possessions, but is happy to talk about his likes and dislikes: for instance, he likes Matisse's *gouaches découpées*, but not the Côte d'Azur odalisques. He hates all the Surrealists except De Chirico. 'I am passionate about Surrealist literature, but definitely not Surrealist painting.' On the other hand, he is very fond of post-war American abstract art: Mark Rothko and Morris Louis, as well as certain Pop artists like Lichtenstein.

In his desire to build a collection in keeping with his own high standards, he

ABOVE Fashion designs using an abstract pattern by the artist Piet Mondrian.

has not bought artworks if he could not afford those he really wanted. His first of many acquisitions with Yves Saint Laurent was a work by Constantin Brancusi, followed by a De Chirico from 1913. Their collection, with a few exceptions, reaches through to the 1960s and the generation of Andy Warhol, who painted several portraits of the fashion designer. There, however, it stops. This may be perceived as a mistake, as there are so many magnificent works in contemporary art, but on this point Pierre Bergé argues quite reasonably that one cannot invest in everything on the same scale. All the same, his involvement in contemporary art is evident through the creative bias of his foundation.

The two friends have always been patrons of the arts, for they have made countless donations to various museums, notably the National Gallery in London and the Pompidou Centre in Paris, before they opened their foundation to the Parisian public in the building that had been the headquarters of the fashion house since 1974, and which they have recently purchased. Thus this beautiful residence, so impregnated with the spirit of Yves Saint Laurent's work, will remain the home of

his art, in which to discover and be inspired by the genius of the master designer. There are no less than five thousand articles of clothing, fifteen thousand accessories, objects, sketches, photographs and videos preserved in the foundation and available for viewing by appointment. The whole collection is made up of the most important pieces of haute couture, together with every single sketch and drawing that Yves Saint Laurent has ever made.

The foundation, which is officially recognized as being of public benefit, also aims to put on exhibitions in all creative fields and to lend support to cultural and educational events. In homage to art and fashion, it has opened its doors with its first exhibition, showing the way in which the designer was influenced by art, and focusing on the links between painting and clothes. Mondrian, Matisse, Braque, Picasso, Bonnard, Léger, Pop artists, Claude Lalanne and various other artists inspired him. The forty-two dresses on display were accompanied by pictures from the Bergé-Saint Laurent collection that provided the models for their designer.

ABOVE On the wall is Picasso's *Still Life with Footstool* (Nature morte au tabouret), 1914.

Far from sinking into the shadows of nostalgia, however, Pierre Bergé wants the foundation to open itself up to the world and to art. In order to achieve this, he is willing to provide the regular revenue that will allow it to operate, and the two friends have also drawn up a will which leaves their collection to the foundation, although they could equally well envisage a massive international sale, with profits going to their new creation in order to finance their artistic and educational projects.

There is a meaning behind such actions. Pierre Bergé has always felt that everyone does what he can in life 'to push back the borders of death: setting up a foundation is the equivalent of other people having children, becoming assassins, writing their name on the stones of Mont Saint Michel…'

A visionary who is also a level-headed businessman, a patron of the arts who is a vain, anarchic perfectionist… What is one to make of Pierre Bergé? As a visionary he is always ready to embark on new projects. To keep up to date, he surrounds himself with young people because, he says, only young people can teach him anything. But no one can tell him how to act or live; he

goes his own way, and he knows just where he is going. He has run the house of Yves Saint Laurent with the utmost skill, without ever losing his human touch.

As a patron, he considers everyone's interests. He is as perfectionist in his choice of art, as he is in his way of life. He is regarded as vain because he is conscious of all that he has achieved and has no illusions about the way people see him: 'I know what I have to do,' he says. 'I accept my own contradictions, I live with them and I'm not afraid to put them on display.' These contradictions would certainly include his being politically left-wing and yet flying in a private plane. All the same, in his everyday life he preserves the memory of his anarchic past, and he has long adopted a saying by André Gide that he finds quite admirable: 'I shall start to grow old on the day that I stop being indignant.'

ABOVE Bergé's workplace.

OPPOSITE Pierre Bergé in front of James Ensor's *The Despair of Pierrot* (Le désespoir de Pierrot), 1892.

DOUBLE PAGE OVERLEAF On the left, two dresses by Claude and Xavier Lalanne, 1969, one in black muslin with a belt of galvanized copper, the other a midnight-blue dress of silk crepe with a girdle of galvanized copper. On the wall behind hangs Henri Matisse's *The Dancer* (Le Danseur), 1937.

Dakis Joannou
THE TRADITIONAL IN THE CONTEMPORARY

Dressed in black from head to toe, avant-garde, yet smiling mischievously with an expression of sparkling joy, Dakis Joannou is a self-confident man who stands at the forefront of those who are spearheading the economic and cultural advance of Greece.

With a passion for architecture and contemporary art, he has succeeded in playing a leading role in the international world of construction, at the same time establishing one of the most prominent centres for contemporary art in Europe. His collection forms the basis of a foundation that has organized exhibitions that are widely considered to be of the highest quality.

Born in Cyprus, Dakis Joannou studied engineering in the United States and then architecture in Italy, before following his family into the construction industry. After his studies and marriage to Lietta in 1970, he embarked on several years of hectic professional activity that took him all over the world. He and his young family spent six years in London, during which time he also travelled to Africa and the Middle East, from Nigeria to Saudi Arabia, and from Dubai to Libya, as these

LEFT Dakis Joannou next to Marcel Duchamp's readymade *Fountain*, 1964.

131

were countries in which the family business was well established. He also returned regularly to its headquarters in Cyprus. In 1980 he moved closer to home and settled his family in Athens, where the business was equally successful. Today, Joannou is at the head of a major construction group and is also director of several companies in different sectors, such as tourism and bottle packaging. He has built several hotels in Greece and has shares in more than twenty companies worldwide.

His white house is situated in a smart, modern area in the hills around Athens, away from the stifling pollution of the city. Protected from prying eyes, it is a very private domain and one cannot help but be charmed by the pure lines of the modern, cubic building, so very different to the remains of ancient Athens nearby. The visitor is welcomed by a Duchamp *Fountain* standing in the entrance. The living room and dining room are both on the first floor, separated by the top of the staircase and by a little wall that does not impede the view into

the space. The whole storey is constructed around an inner courtyard which recalls the light and airy layout of traditional Greek houses. On the other side, the living room opens out onto a large terrace and a deep blue swimming pool where a Jeff Koons sculpture of white marble, representing the artist and his former wife, stands out against the vivid colour of the water. On the walls of the living room are two large painted canvases by Ofili, and opposite is Dakis's favourite intimate corner, with armchairs and a low table, watched over by a huge Liza Lou sculpture of a voluptuous African-American woman, who might have stepped straight out of a Harlem disco club. An old table of rare wood, covered with objects and family photographs, provides a link with the past.

In the basement, as on a ship, you have to walk along a passageway to get to a large room containing monumental works by Jeff Koons and Ofili: from there you go into a vast reception room with a bar, where Sue Webster and Tim Noble's 'prehistoric couple' are confronted by Robert Gober's white sink and Tom Sachs's hanging planes.

There are installations by Robert Gober and Jeff

ABOVE The dining room is dominated by Michael Bevilacquas's huge painting *Shut Up, I'm Meditatin'*, 1999.

OPPOSITE Dakis Joannou below Tom Sachs's *Two Boeing 767s*, 2001.

Koons all over the house, among the works of other great contemporary artists such as Maurizio Cattelan, Christopher Wool and Vanessa Beecroft. There is an added charm in the fact that each work fits in so naturally with its setting that it seems to have always been there. But this belies the truth, for Joannou in fact changes the decor every so often in order to surround himself with other items from his collection.

Dakis Joannou has always been interested in art, but did not have the time to indulge his interest until his return to Greece. He liked the idea of becoming a collector, although he did not really know what was involved or even how to begin. To begin with, he bought a few works without actually trying to build up a collection, simply with the aim of living among things that he liked and that would decorate his house. He was already collecting works by famous artists during the 1980s, but later he wanted to become properly

involved in the art world. It was at this time that he happened to have lunch with the French art critic, founder and theorist of Nouveau Réalisme, Pierre Restany, who suggested that he should set up a foundation. Dakis was so delighted with the idea that in 1983 he did just that, naming it the Deste Foundation.

One of the first exhibitions held by the foundation was in Geneva, with the participation of Andelina von Fürstenberg, who was then director of the city's Centre d'Art Contemporain. Together they then organized a new exhibition in Cyprus, which was followed by two more in Greece. In due course, exhibitions entitled 'Cultural Geometry' (1988), 'Artificial Nature' (1990) and 'Post Human' (1993) were organized in Athens and presented at Cyprus House, because the foundation did not as yet have premises of its own. These and subsequent shows aimed to support certain publishing projects concerned with the relations between art and

ABOVE Jeff Koons, *Bourgeois Bust – Jeff and Ilona*, 1991.

contemporary culture. For the most part, these exhibitions were directed by Jeffrey Deitch, Joannou's trusted adviser, and by Greek organizers such as Helena Papadopoulos, Catherine Cafopoulos and Haris Savopoulos.

In the mid 1980s, however, Joannou changed his approach. In 1985, on a trip to New York, he met Jeff Koons. Seeing his work, the collector considered buying a piece but, as he recalls, 'I didn't want to buy it without knowing what it was. After a long conversation with Jeff and having realized how totally committed he was, I bought the work from him, and later many others. I now have about thirty works of his.'

Since he was doing a lot of business in the United States, Joannou spent a good deal of time in New York, and began to invest in art in a manner that was very different to that required by the foundation. He went to sales and galleries,

ABOVE Glass beads are the favourite material of the American artist Liza Lou, *Super Sister*, 1999.

and began to put together a collection. He also met Robert Gober, whose work he greatly admires, and bought several pieces which are now among his most prized items. He also acquired several works by Maurizio Cattelan.

Joannou's wife Lietta, a Cypriot like himself, has always supported him, even if she is not quite so involved. They exchange ideas and have long conversations about contemporary art and artists.

When Dakis Joannou started collecting in earnest, the Deste Foundation changed its character, and since then its activities have tended to be organized mainly around the collection, although this was not in fact an integral part of the foundation itself. The exhibitions displayed items from the collection along different thematic lines, such as the famous 'Everything That's Interesting is New' and 'Shortcuts'. Thanks to these exhibitions, the Dakis Joannou Collection became well known for its focus on the artists of the 1980s and their

neo-conceptual approach. What they had in common was their work on the aesthetics of consumerism, the economics of the art market, and the deconstruction of value systems, often returning to the Duchamp concept of the readymade, now invested with a narrative and symbolic quality.

In 1998, the Deste Foundation acquired an old paper factory to set up a centre that would make contemporary art more accessible to the general public. Entrance to the foundation is free of charge, and it also gives young artists the opportunity to have their work exhibited. Dakis Joannou wants to initiate a dialogue between the generations, especially by organizing exhibitions that combine emerging artists with those who are more established, and also by bringing together organizers from different generations. What he is actually trying to create is a kind of competitive

spirit that will benefit everyone, including himself: 'With contemporary art you are at the heart of a dialogue on art,' he says. 'That is why I want a foundation that will be as public as possible, because I want to take part in exchanges and discussions on the art of today.'

While he is eager to forge links between generations, he is above all interested in the evolution of art from the moment of its creation, and his collection is becoming more and more focused on this aspect. He has abandoned certain themes, and has sold some items in order to acquire others that strengthen the themes he is pursuing, so that his collection of some three hundred works is made all the more coherent. His interest has always been contemporary art, and this is the direction in which he continues to advance. Recently he sold a picture by Ed Ruscha in order to buy more avant-garde pieces, and with the money he raised from the sale he was able to acquire some twenty works

by young artists. In this way he is fostering creativity and also discovering new talent.

The Deste Foundation, like Joannou's own collection, is playing an important role in bringing Greece onto the international art scene, and this is a responsibility that he takes very seriously. By establishing the Deste Prize in 1999, awarded to a young Greek artist every other year, the foundation has fulfilled one of its main purposes: to promote contemporary art in Greece and to support young Greek artists.

There are three main creative themes that correspond to the aesthetic make-up of the collection and offer a guideline to the artists: relations between national identities and international realities, contemporary reality in Greece, and the problem of individual identity. In order to provide a balance between local and international tastes, there are two groups of judges: a committee of people from the Greek art world – collectors, curators, art critics, etc. – who choose the six finalists from around fifty candidates, and secondly an international panel of art professionals who select the winner. The prize has so far been awarded three times, and each time the winner has been a woman: Panayota Tzamourani in 1999, who took part in the exhibition 'New Trends in Contemporary Greek Art', organized by Dan Cameron in that year, Georgia Sagri in 2001, and Maria Papadimitrou in 2003.

With the same aim of promoting the Greek art scene, Dakis Joannou also mounted a major exhibition of his collection in 2004, to coincide with the Olympic Games in Athens: among the participants in 'Monument to Now' were Dan Cameron, Jeffrey Deitch, Nancy Spector, Alison M. Gingeras and Massimiliano Gioni, along with many other major

ABOVE In the centre, part of Urs Fischer's life-size female wax candle tryptich *What if the phone rings*, 2003; above are Tom Sachs's 'Boeings'. On the left, just in view, is Tim Noble and Sue Webster's light-bulb installation *Ye$*, 2001.

figures from the current international art world. The exhibition brought together about sixty of the most influential artists over the last ten years, as well as the most recent innovations, incorporating a wide variety of approaches, including those of Paul McCarthy, Pipillotti Rist, Anna Gaskell, Chen Zen, Gabriel Orozco, Gilbert & George, and Lina Theodorou. To ensure that international collectors were there, Joannou chartered a plane to bring them from the Basel art fair to see the exhibition and attend the various arts events.

In parallel to his work with the foundation, Dakis Joannou is involved with various museums, most notably the Solomon R. Guggenheim Museum in New York, where he is a member of the acquisitions committee for contemporary art, and also chairman of the museum's international board. He not only supports the museum and raises funds, but also maintains control over decisions, since it is a tradition that the curators choose works in conjunction with the acquisitions committee, while each purchase is initially voted on by the board of trustees, who thus have a very real say in the future of the Guggenheim.

Dakis Joannou does not know exactly what will become of the foundation or his collection, but he often thinks about it: 'For me, a collection must be a living thing. I continually change it, and I shall go on developing it. It's therefore very strange if someone wants, for instance, to build his own museum, because that stops the whole process. I'm completely against it unless you have the means to endow the museum with sufficient funds for it eventually to become a MoMA.'

Dakis Joannou could have acted like a mogul, but instead he has remained modest and faithful to the deeper values of family and friendship. He is a public figure who likes to keep his personal life private. Avant-garde he may be, but he has remained sensitive to his origins in adapting modernity to Greek tradition.

Today he is a major collector on the international scene, and is considered to be a barometer of tastes and trends in contemporary art. Through his commitment to his country and abilityto think globally, he has helped Greece enormously to open up to the world of art. and be significant on the international stage.

OPPOSITE In the foreground, to the left, is Jeff Koons's famous ceramic sculpture *Michael Jackson and Bubbles*, 1988. In the background is the installation *Masters of the Universe*, 1998-2000, by Tim Noble and Sue Webster.

Angela Rosengart
PORTRAITS OF A COLLECTOR

Picasso loved Angela Rosengart so much that he did five portraits of her in succession. The muse that he captured in these paintings has scarcely changed, even though she is now in her seventies: the elegance of her heart shines out from the elongated face, the hair is pulled back, the eyes are wide and deep, and the gentle smile at the corners of her mouth invites you into a dialogue. She is full of wit and subtle humour, tactful and yet at the same time strong – a woman of taste and conviction.

The other true portrait of this great collector, art dealer and most recently museum director consists in the works that are so much a part of her. Born into an upper-class Swiss family in Lucerne, she could easily have settled into the comfortable existence that was more or less forced upon her in 1948 when her father, Siegfried Rosengart, an art dealer, asked her to help him run the business after he suffered a skiing accident. She was just sixteen years old, but she threw herself into the task. She was certainly precocious: three years earlier she had discovered the work of Paul Klee, when her father organized a retrospective with the artist's widow, and two years later she had bought some for herself – her first collection. Her father sensibly instructed her in the basics: only to buy works that she liked, and above all not to buy anything for the sake of short-term business. This was the nature of the passion that he instilled in Angela, and she proved highly adept, while their likes and dislikes were so in tune, that by the time she was twenty-five he had appointed her co-director of the gallery. Also in common was their shared conviction that one must always hold on to any work whose true value is not appreciated by the collectors. In her own words: 'If collectors were so blind that they could not see the quality of the work, then they did not deserve to own it. And so I kept it. The art lovers could always come running.'

In the end, through a combination of sheer hard work, discernment and passion, the Rosengarts had assembled more than two hundred works of outstanding quality which, quite unintentionally,

LEFT A room in the Rosengart Collection: On the far wall is Fernand Léger's *Contrast of Forms* (Contraste de formes), 1913; and on the far left is Picasso's *Still Life with Guitar* (Nature morte à la guitare), 1922.

ABOVE (left) The façade of the Rosengart Collection in Lucerne, and (right) Angela Rosengart in front of Picasso's *Portrait of Angela*.

covered the entire history of art from the late 19th century: Monet, Renoir, Pissarro, Seurat, Cézanne, Vuillard, Bonnard, Matisse, Braque, Kandinsky, Modigliani, Utrillo, Soutine, Miró, Léger, Rouault, and above all Picasso and Klee. The private Rosengart collection of Klee is one of the most comprehensive in the world, and through it one can follow the evolution of his work from beginning to end.

As for Picasso, while the Basel Kunstmuseum and the Beyeler collections concentrate on his early work, the Rosengart collection focuses on his later art, which is nowadays held to be of major importance, though at the time when the Rosengarts embraced it so passionately – twenty years before everyone else – it was considered puzzling. Quite simply they loved the humour and irony in the late work of Picasso, who at the end of his life was more than ever free from all constraints.

In 1978, to celebrate the 800th jubilee of Lucerne, Siegfried and Angela Rosengart donated eight of Picasso's masterpieces to the town, and twenty years later she gave the artist's portraits of her to the museum, as well as two hundred photographs by the American David Douglas Duncan. In 1981 the collectors were awarded the prestigious Epingle d'honneur, which is given to outstanding benefactors of the town.

Today, Angela Rosengart travels all over the world, but Lucerne is still her base, where she leads a relatively simple life. She is more at home in a discreet little hotel in Graubünden than she is in the prestigious and luxurious places that she could so easily frequent. She detests ostentation, and loves the beauty of people, objects and works of art. Although she is self-taught, her knowledge of modern art is of course immense; nor has she neglected the Old Masters. Her taste in music extends from Monteverdi and Schubert to Bartók and Stravinsky, and in literature she loves reading Shakespeare (in English), and Giraudoux for his humour. In 2003, she was awarded an honorary doctorate by the University of Zürich.

On her father's death in 1985, when Angela Rosengart was fifty-three years old, she decided to

ABOVE Picasso is everywhere: *Dawn Serenade* (L'Aubade), 1967.

OPPOSITE (above) The former board room of the Banque Nationale, which has been preserved in its original state from 1924; and (below) behind the visitors are three works by Paul Klee from 1923, from left to right: *Harmony Blue Orange* (Harmonie bleue orange), *Eros* and *Double Tent*.

set up a foundation that would benefit all art lovers. At the end of March 2003, the foundation was finally opened to the public. It is situated near the station, the Musée des Beaux-Arts and the Palais des Congrès. A simple, elegant building, it dominates the main street, and was originally the old Banque Nationale Suisse, designed in 1924 by the Zürich architect Hermann Herter. The conversion was carried out by Roger Diener, himself a collector, who is well known for his successful work on the architectural museum in Basel and the Galleria Nazionale d'Arte Moderna in Rome. Angela Rosengart found in him the ideal partner to capture the essential spirit of the project. She spent many long days telling him about the history of the works in the collection, so that he could grasp the entire context and provide the perfect setting. The understanding between collector and architect was so complete that each work of art was given exactly the right position in a space that has been specially conceived, designed and constructed for it.

Through her enterprise and adoration of beautiful things, Angela Rosengart is internationally recognized as one of the great friends of the arts. She leads a full life, devoted to what she considers to be the finest aspects of human civilization. Picasso was right when he paid tribute in one of his portraits to the simple but great lady in the red shawl, around whom he placed a garland of vine leaves. The photograph taken by Jacqueline Picasso which shows the painter dancing around his collector says it all – a wonderful relationship between artist and art-loving patron, filled with mutual respect: they are complementary partners, both in their way indispensable, one might say, to the happiness of others.

LEFT (above) Through the glass door, Picasso's *Standing Nude and Seated Man with Pipe* (Nue debout et homme à la pipe assis), 1968; and (below) a painting from Picasso's Cubist period, *Le violon au café*, 1913.

ABOVE RIGHT Marc Chagall's paint palette.

DOUBLE PAGE OVERLEAF In the former vaults of the Banque Nationale Suisse there are now one hundred and twenty works by Paul Klee.

Uli and Rita Sigg
WHEN CHINA AWAKES

Uli Sigg is ambassador to the world for contemporary Chinese art. His successful international career has made him into a pioneering go-between, as respected in China as he is in the West for his accomplishments in the fields of economics and art. He studied law in Zürich, but chance led him to take up a post as economics editor for the Swiss publisher Ringier, of which he is now vice-president. He quickly decided that he wanted to become active himself in the economic sphere, and so he began a career in industry with the firm of Schindler, who specialize in making lifts. This gave him an early opportunity to work in the field of exports, and later he became an administrative adviser, working especially with the Chinese.

In 1980 he set up the first joint venture with China, which until then had been completely closed to the West. Knowing that China had to prove to the world that one could safely and successfully invest in this vast country, Uli Sigg became a pioneer in establishing commercial relations that were to be a model for the rest of the world. Ever present on the international scene, he continued to implement new ideas –

LEFT View of the Siggs's estate.

149

for instance, a joint chamber of commerce between Switzerland and China.

Uli Sigg grew up near Lucerne, surrounded by the work of 19th-century Swiss artists such as Hodler and Anker, but as a young man he was not so impressed. It took him some twenty years before he discovered contemporary art through a friend and collector. Initially, he was fascinated by Surrealism, buying his first painting from a local artist, and then by abstract art, although it took him a while to get to grips with it.

He still loves to surround himself with art which at first seems strange to him. During the 1970s and 1980s, depending on where his various business trips took him, he would buy works by contemporary artists such as Gerhard Richter, Gotthard Graubner and Rachel Whiteread – the last western artists to be found in the Sigg Collection, to be precise, in the office of his wife. The collection that they have since put together is still contemporary, but it is now predominantly Chinese.

In 1990, Uli Sigg left Schindler to work for various companies which included Ringier. By now he was so familiar with China, and so competent in his dealings with the people, that in 1994 he was appointed Swiss ambassador to China, North Korea and Mongolia. He and his wife thought it over for three days, before accepting this new challenge. The appointment opened up entirely new perspectives for them: it was a unique opportunity to get to know China and its art. During his previous visits, Uli had gained some knowledge of contemporary Chinese art, but now he would be able to follow its development from the late 1970s, but particularly from 1986 through to the present day.

Before China was opened to the West, the only exhibitions were of figurative art, either traditional or of the 'socialist realist' variety, designed to promote political propaganda and rigidly controlled by the State. Against this background, contemporary artists were only gradually able to gain access to western art, and they took time to become familiar with it. By imitating Impressionism, Expressionism and post-war

LEFT Through the open door, Zhang Huan's *My New York*, 1995.

OVERLEAF, LEFT: Above the door hangs *Duchamp's Retrospective Exhibition*, 2000/01, by Shi Xinning, and inside the room, on the far wall, is Yan Lei's *The Curators*, 2000.

OVERLEAF, RIGHT View of the staircase, beyond which is Hai Bo's picture *They No. 3*, 1999. To the left of the door is the large-scale *Bloodline Series*, 1998, by Zhang Xiaogang.

151

American art, in time they learned to find a mode of expression that suited them as artists in their own right.

In 1995, the couple began their new lives as ambassadors to Beijing, and became more and more involved with the works that were emerging from the contemporary Chinese art scene. Rita Sigg often acted as an intermediary between the artists and the collector, for the couple were determined to get to know and understand the artists as they made their way through the various provinces. In China at that time, works of art were being bought and sold through friends and personal contacts, for there were no galleries or dealers as such. So you might discover an artist at an improvised exhibition, for example, and then through meeting others gradually expand your circle of contacts. Accordingly, so-called market prices were arbitrary, and some artists were taking the greatest western painters as their financial yardsticks.

So the utmost diplomacy

was required when it came to negotiating, in a manner that has no equivalent in the West. The situation was made all the more delicate by the fact that most of these artists lived in appalling conditions: it was a different world, although now, as in so many other aspects of Chinese society, things have changed, and the present quality of life for creative people is closer to that of their western counterparts. China learns very quickly.

The quest for contemporary art led up and down many staircases and across many courtyards, but it enriched the collection of the Siggs, who by now were known to such Swiss curators as Harald Szeemann and Peter Pakesch. At Uli's invitation they came to China to seek his advice, along with other major figures from the international art world. Now an expert on the subject, Uli Sigg decided in 1988 to set up a prize, the CCAA (Contemporary Chinese Art Award), which he organized and financed himself. He had to be very diplomatic, because contemporary art was mostly being

ABOVE Staircase with four works by Zhou Tiehai.

criticized and condemned, or at the very least ignored by official Chinese institutions and the government. And so careful thought had to be given as to how to make the work accessible to international curators, and the world in general, without endangering the artists. The creation of a prize brought with it the opportunity to identify and list the contemporary artists at work in China. The jury for this biennial prize consists of six curators and others from the art world, half of whom are Chinese, thereby legitimizing a project that was initiated by the West. There is no action that does not leave a memory, and a catalogue features the works of the winners from 1998 to 2002. Soon, positive results were emerging: Harald Szeemann, who has twice been a member of the jury, mounted the first exhibition of artists from China at the 1999 Venice Biennale, providing them with a wonderful opportunity to present their art to a western public increasingly interested in their country. Once again, it was Uli Sigg who had built a bridge between China and the West.

This interest had long since manifested itself in the Sigg Collection, which contains some one thousand two hundred works by almost one hundred and seventy artists employing all kinds of media: painting, sculpture, installations, photographs and videos. Some had already achieved success in the West, through living in the United States or Europe, particularly in France.

The majority of these artists living abroad have adopted a certain strategy with regard to the western eye, which is not so accustomed to other kinds of art but appreciates the newness of it, especially when it comes from China. These artists have not only adapted their approach but, since the international market has provided access to such art, some are even able to

ABOVE The large drawing room. On the floor in the foreground is the wooden sculpture *Map of China*, 2003, by Al Wei Wei, beyond which are the vases *Whitewash*, 1995-2000, in front of the window. To the left is a picture by Luo Hui, 1999, and to the right is *Portrait (No. 16)*, 1998/99, by Yang Shaobin.

command hundreds of thousands of dollars for their work. The downside of this is that the globalization of art could potentially dilute authentic Chinese forms of expression by incorporating them into the mainstream. As for the artists who remain in China, their principal ambition is to be seen and appreciated for their art alone, without continual reference to their origin.

Contemporary Chinese art, which the western art world has access to, can be divided into two main categories. On the one hand there are those works that can easily be understood by anyone who has a limited knowledge of their context: they deal with human subject matter or situations that might arise anywhere in the world, so there is no need for them to be viewed in relation to their Chinese origins. The other category comprises those works which, if they are to be understood and appreciated, require awareness of the context which has given rise to, and illuminates their content. For instance, a political work based on the law that forbids couples to have more than one child would only be comprehensible to someone who actually knew that such a law existed.

Uli Sigg very soon realized that neither the Chinese people nor their institutions were collecting this art. When he began his collection in 1988, no one else had the money, space or desire to do so: he and his wife were the only ones interested in visiting the artists, and they went to see as many as possible, in total about one thousand. They were shown all kinds of works: paintings, depictions of the Cultural Revolution, and also posters and wood engravings from that period. In this respect, the Sigg Collection is now of major historical interest, for it reflects, even for the Chinese government, the crucial stages from which contemporary China has emerged. It is therefore not surprising that today the Chinese themselves are trying to negotiate with this experienced and successful collector for the return of his works to China.

The Siggs live on an impressive 16th-century estate not far from Lucerne, which offers a perfect setting for the meeting between the western art world and that of

ABOVE, LEFT TO RIGHT the porcelain sculpture *Boy reading Maobook*, 1998/99, by Xu Yihui; and the sculpture *No. 2 Materialis*, 2001, by Wang Guangyi.

OPPOSITE Uli Sigg's office. The burned books in the fireplace are by Xu Yihui; and Shi Yong's figures on the mantelpiece represent *The new image of Shanghai Today*, 1999.

contemporary China. They receive national and international delegations, always in the hope of creating a platform in the West for the Chinese artists to whom the collector has given so much support, commuting as he does between the two worlds and often spending months at a time in China. He is in an ideal position to establish vital contacts that will bring together artists, curators and journalists who would not otherwise have access to this distant land. Museums like the Kunsthalle in Basel, the museum of art in Berne, and the Hamburger Bahnhof in Berlin have already held exhibitions of some of the artists in his collection, giving them yet another opportunity to further their cause and to enter into new dialogues that would not be possible in their own country.

If China becomes a superpower politically and economically, it is not impossible that contemporary Chinese art might also gain in stature. With the support of his wife, and with all his talents as a businessman, diplomat and collector, Uli Sigg, will have performed a double service to China and the West.

LEFT In the foreground, a group of figures entitled *Opening Ceremony*, 2002, by Li Zhanyang; behind them is *Untitled*, 1998, by Fang Lijun.

DOUBLE PAGE OVERLEAF The Siggs in their barn, among a group of twenty-five wooden sculptures, *2000 AD*, by Yue Minjun.

159

Thomas Olbricht
THE ENERGY OF ART

Thomas Olbricht grew up in the German country-side, in a family of entrepreneurs. After studying chemistry in Marburg and then in Bochum, where he wrote his doctoral thesis, he studied medicine in Essen, specializing in endocrinology, the science of hormones.

Initially a university professor, in 1994 he opened a state-of-the-art research clinic in the Ruhr basin. In 2001, however, he decided to sell his highly successful practice to devote himself mainly to art. During his childhood, when he had collected stamps and matchboxes, Olbricht had already realized that he was a collector at heart, but it was finally through conversations with his great-uncle Karl Ströher, one of the best known and most prominent collectors of post-war American and German art, that he graduated towards the world of art.

The key moment in his collecting career was a meeting with Joseph Beuys at a time when the artist was not yet a major figure. When he was still a student, Olbricht went to the opening of the Landesmuseum in Darmstadt, to which Karl Ströher had made a permanent loan of most of his Beuys collection, including the famous *Block*. The exhibition caused an indignant stir among the invited guests. Today the scandal, which to a degree was also political, has become part of art history, but this experience set Olbricht thinking, and no doubt inspired his later desire to become involved in contemporary art, the more provocative the better.

It was not until he was thirty-six years old, however, that he really set out to build a proper collection, initially using his savings of DM 1000 before he inherited enough money to tackle the task in earnest. Self-taught, he went as often as possible to museums and exhibitions, to train his eye. He acquired a number of works locally, and soon began to concentrate mainly on Art Informel and abstract art, especially the works of

LEFT The entrance hall. On the left is a baroque cupboard with ivory intarsia; in front of the staircase is a sculpture by Gustav Kluge; and on the wall, as you walk down the stairs, is Gerhard Richter's large-scale *Abstract Picture* (Abstraktes Bild), 1989.

ABOVE, CENTRE Erich Heckels' *Standing Child (Fränzi standing)* (Stehendes Kind, Fränzi stehend), 1910; and a sculpture by Stephan Balkenhol. Also, a Mother and Child sculpture.

ABOVE RIGHT Thomas Olbricht in his office. In the background is Heckels' coloured woodcut *White Horses* (Weisse Pferde), 1912; below are various bronze sculptures by Renée Sintenis. On the desk is a wooden skull as a *memento mori*.

DOUBLE PAGE OVERLEAF The drawing room. At the back is Joseph Marioni's large *Yellow Painting*, 1996. On the right-hand wall are two pictures by Thomas Scheibitz: *Untitled (Bird)* (Ohne Titel [Vogel]) and *1492 (Houses)* (1492 [Häuser]), both 2002. Between them is Andreas Slominski's *Rat Trap (Church)* (Rattenfalle [Kirche]), 1998. On the easel is a photographic work *Marilyn*, 1990/91, by Philip-Lorca Di Corcia.

post-war German artists such as Willy Baumeister, Fritz Winter and above all Ernst Wilhelm Nay.

Vibrant colours, dynamism and lasting quality are all crucial factors in his choice of art. His particular interest in the paintings of Ernst Wilhelm Nay brought him into contact with Elisabeth Scheibler Nay, the artist's widow. Such was his intensity that in the early 1990s, if anyone wanted to buy one of the artist's works at a fair, the reply would always be: 'Very sorry, but Olbricht has bought it.' At that time he had thirty-five of the artist's major works, but only three of these remain now, together with several works on paper.

Thomas Olbricht's meeting in 1995 with Wolfgang Schoppmann, director of a small auction house of contemporary art, was another decisive moment, for he was the first to auction works by Joseph Beuys. Schoppmann was to play a major role in the development of the Olbricht Collection, which was to acquire an international reputation. Initially focusing on

LEFT A bouquet of flowers on the table brings a breath of nature into this minimalist home. On the wall is *Yellow Balloon* (Gelber Ballon), 1998, by Gisela Bullacher.

ABOVE RIGHT On the baroque chest of drawers are various Art Nouveau vases by Daum and Gallé.

German Art Informel, a year later he decided on a complete change of direction. He again met with Schoppmann, who began by offering pieces that did not appeal. But when he suggested works by the post-war German artists such as Gerhard Richter, the young collector responded enthusiastically and bought them without hesitation. Today his collection contains important works from throughout Richter's career.

The collection began to take on its own impetus: Olbricht increasingly became an expert on contemporary art and amassed nearly two thousand works, covering each generation, and including women artists such as Marlène Dumas, Sarah Morris and Lisa Ruyter. His collection encompassed one hundred and eighty artists, employing all kinds of media: painting, engraving, sculpture, video, installations, and especially photography, with particular emphasis on Cindy Sherman – eighty photographs ranging from her *Untitled Film Stills* series to *Clown Photos*, one of the most complete series to be found in any private collection. There were other artist-photographers who also attracted Olbricht's attention: Jeff Wall, Thomas Demand, Andreas Gursky, Andres Serrano, Nan

167

Goldin, Matthew Barney and the Dutch artist Rineke Dijkstra. So great was his interest in art photography and video that during the 1990s he became one of the leading collectors in the field, sometimes shocking his guests who were used to more conventional art forms. But Professor Olbricht always seemed to be ahead of others, and this also applies to his other passion: the woodcuts of the German Expressionists known as Die Brücke, especially those of Ernst Ludwig Kirchner.

He wanted a living collection that would continue to evolve, as it did when he became interested in new artists such as Kiki Smith, John Isaacs, Katharina Fritsch and others who were dealing with issues of death, failure, loss, ephemera and, in contrast, a lust for life. No doubt his reflections on these subjects also led him to acquire a number of *memento mori* from the late Middle Ages through to modern times.

The first time his works went on public display was in the year 2000 in Bremen, where particular note was taken of the references to sexuality, violence, the human body and the *memento mori*. It was striking that half the artists in the collection were women, and their works were also exhibited successfully in 2002 at the Gl. Holtegaard Foundation near Copenhagen. More recently, the Olbricht Collection worked with the Folkwang Museum in Essen, to present a room of variations on the theme of 'moving energies'. Unlike other collectors, Thomas Olbricht has no desire to s et up a foundation, but wants the public to enjoy his acquisitions: for example, he has made a permanent loan of a large sculpture and mural by Thomas Schütte to the new philharmonic society in Essen.

His own home has been built around the collection. There, with his wife Claudia and two children, he installs objects from his 'great treasure of art', constantly varying the delights. Above all, he is a collector who does not think twice, who is committed to contemporary art, but at the same time never loses touch with the foundations of his collection: German Expressionism, the *memento mori,* and his *objets d'art.* They all reflect the infectious enthusiasm of an art lover who spreads his love to everyone around him.

RIGHT The pet dog Nuggy stands guard over Jochen Hiltmann's *Burst Ball* (Aufgebrochene Kugel), 1964.

Beth Rudin DeWoody
THE UNINHIBITED COLLECTOR

When you meet Beth Rudin DeWoody for the first time, you are reminded of the young Liza Minnelli, with her black hair cut fashionably short, her sparkling eyes, and original clothes. She has a unique style and a rounded personality that enables her to talk to anyone and everyone. Her expansive gestures underline an immense enthusiasm, and the slightly raucous voice says everything about her passion and resolve.

The interior of her home is just like the woman herself, at the same time very feminine and very sophisticated. She is a highly intelligent person with a large number of books filling her home. Her bright apartment looks out onto the Hudson, and consists of rooms that are filled with human warmth. There you will find artworks of all kinds – in particular, many works on paper. The entrance hall is decorated with drawings, engravings, and 20th-century photographs. When you enter the living room, you are initially bowled over by the panoramic view of the river, but then your eye swiftly turns to a collection of glassware in vivid greens standing on a table beside a sofa covered with leopard-spotted cushions. In one corner is a grand piano adorned with pictures by Tom Sachs and Sylvie Fleury, and there are more pictures on the opposite wall, while sculptures of bones and skulls in different materials are casually lying around in a basket on the floor and on a low table.

In the Art Deco dining room, the large table holds Jeff Koons's famous 'train', and the biggest wall in the room contains an impressive number of vintage photographs by artists from all over the world. The passage leading to the bedrooms is also full of photographs, with portraits of film stars and images from the fashion world.

Beth Rudin DeWoody has always lived in an artistic environment. She grew up in New York where she, her brother and cousins all attended the Rudolf Steiner School. Here children were encouraged to practise the plastic arts throughout their education. This naturally made her sensitive to the world of creativity, and indeed she has always been a collector, having begun at an early age with her brother to 'accumulate' magazines. 'One

LEFT In the distant passage one can see a portrait of Gladys Begelman (Beth's mother) by Alex Katz.

ABOVE LEFT In the dining room is Jeff Koons's *Jim Beam – J. B. Turner Train*, 1986;

RIGHT The collector.

171

day', she recalls, 'my mother threw out my entire collection of *Chilli* magazines, which were certainly collectors' items… I just went crazy!'

She always loved things that were original and different. The family itself was seriously into culture. Although her father was not a collector as such, art occupied a very important place in his life, and he actively supported the cause by buying artworks. When her mother went to live in California with her second husband, she too discovered the local artists and built up a fine collection of works by artists such as McCracken and Davis. Beth's aunt and uncle also collected art, and had a considerable influence on her.

When the family's three foundations merged as the Samuel Rudin Family Foundation, Beth became a member and then director, as she remains today. The foundation exists for the benefit of museums, education and music, and it enables Beth to play a full part in New York's cultural life. She is also passionate about music and is involved with the

New York Music Academy. In 1985, she was invited to join the acquisitions committee for engravings at the Whitney Museum and then at the Museum of Modern Art, again placing her right in the heart of the artistic and cultural scene, where she continues to flourish, for she has always demonstrated a rich combination of flair, perseverance and imagination.

Having studied anthropology at Santa Barbara, Beth returned to New York before spending some time working in Africa. In 1975 she married Jim, a painter, and together they used to buy *objets d'art* at the flea market – some paintings, but mainly engravings from the 1920s and 1930s, especially by Carol Clock and Pearl Andecker. During those years, her eye and judgment gradually grew sharper, not least because she was living with an artist. 'We started by collecting works from the fifties,' she says, 'which were not in vogue at the time and were therefore a lot cheaper,' but they also collected the work of young artists, most of whom were their personal friends.

If you ask her how she goes about making a purchase, she will tell you that basically it's a matter of wandering around and then stopping when something catches her eye. Generally, it will be in a 'modernist style'. She likes things that are 'visually strong' – the Russian Constructivists, for example, although she does not actually collect them. But she also learns from other people. Beth and Jim became close friends of David Keel, initially curator of the drawings and engravings department in New York's Metropolitan Museum and now at the Whitney Museum, and in the 1980s they also got to know Nathan Coladner, director of the Emmerich Gallery, who introduced them to works from the 1940s and 1950s. Similarly, through the dealer Robert Monk, Beth became friends with the Des Meltiv family, wonderful collectors with whom she visited galleries, artists' studios and major exhibitions. She was deeply impressed by their knowledge of the art world, and by the manner in which they would stop every minute in order to greet someone. This, she says, was the kind of person she dreamed of becoming. Her dream has come true. 'Now I'm like them – I know everyone on the art scene,' she laughs.

Nowadays she buys a lot from the daughter of the Des Meltiv family,

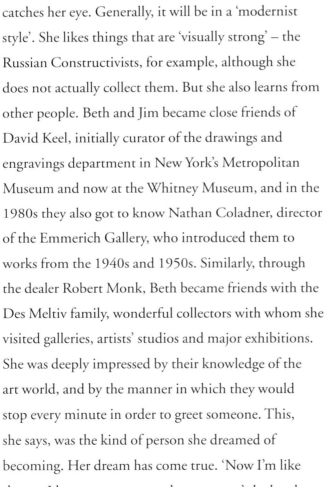

RIGHT The large dining table with Koons's *Jim Bean – J. B. Turner Train*.

who runs a very fine gallery of contemporary art in New York. There she has found work by the Scottish artist Norah Flanagan, and work by Johnny Dickinson. In fact it was after her divorce that she really began in earnest to collect the things she liked, and it was then that she began to delve deeper into contemporary art, trusting in the specialists who had first introduced her to it. She owes her collection of photographs to Bruce Spelly, a Toronto dealer who showed her the work of Ryan McFinley, initiating a lasting passion. During the 1990s she discovered the artist Tom Sachs, from whom she bought a great deal, being equally enamoured by his work and personality. They soon became great friends.

In the early days, she did not necessarily buy iconic works, and even today she will only buy things that really appeal to her personally, particularly drawings. She will very proudly inform you, for example, that she has recently found a marvellous classical drawing by Julien Verdier,

ABOVE On the grand piano is *Pradavalue Meal*, 1998, by Tom Sachs.

but at the same time she tends to favour and promote the work of young artists. In fact one cannot label her, for she does not confine herself to one particular style. If she had to define the general tenor of her collection, she would say it was 'post-Pop'. In this context, she is particularly fond of Sylvie Fleury, Thomas Hirschhorn and Tom Sachs, and she has recently bought a photograph by Thomas Ruff. She does not allow herself to be confined to any one category of art, and will stop at no geographical borders, for she has works by Russian, Japanese, European, and of course American artists. She knows no limits, and this freedom fuels her collector's passion.

Nowadays she remains busy running the family foundation, acting as a consultant for *Hamptons Magazine*, and sitting on the architectural committee of the Whitney Museum. With her always convincing manner, Beth Rudin DeWoody has transmitted her passion to her children, whom she takes with her to art fairs all over the world, including the annual

contemporary art fair in Basel, the Venice Biennale, and the Kassel Documenta. No important exhibition of contemporary art or design escapes her, and both her son and daughter have developed a real taste for art, starting collections of their own. 'We're surrounded by art and music,' she says, 'and that's in keeping with the family tradition.' Since he was very young, her son has been building up an intriguing collection, and as his taste rapidly develops, he does not hesitate to sell works he has just acquired in order to replace them with others that he finds more interesting. His mother, on the other hand, great collector that she is, obviously has a more focused eye and knows exactly what direction she wishes to take. She very rarely sells her acquisitions.

Beth Rudin DeWoody does not yet know what will become of her collection. At the moment her son likes the idea of a permanent home for his mother's drawings, but she herself is busy cataloguing them, and then she will see.

Always committed, she is ever ready to lend support to the art world and to promote education through art. She regards this as a duty, especially in the United States, where art remains very elitist. The great individual collectors are moulding the future of the arts by establishing foundations, making substantial donations to public institutions, and helping the artists of their day in order to make up for the State's lack of support – a situation that Beth considers disgraceful. She cannot and will not accept that, she loves her art and her artists, and will go on fighting for them and for the art-going public.

ABOVE A seated figure by Anissa Mac, 1998.

DOUBLE PAGE OVERLEAF
The brightly-lit living room.

Frank Cohen
THE CHARLES SAATCHI OF THE NORTH

Frank Cohen was born in the north of England in Manchester, the second most important city after London, and a place once renowned for its cotton mills. Following the decline and eventual disappearance of textile manufacturing in the 1950s, the city has since recovered so that it now manufactures half of the products created in Britain today.

For sixty years, Frank Cohen has remained faithful to this rough-edged city. An only child whose parents were older than most, his first experience of the arts was at the age of seven, when a neighbour introduced him to the world of classical music. Later, while still at school, he began to collect cards from cigarette packs, exchanging them with other enthusiasts until he possessed a complete set.

At the beginning of the 1960s, when he was still only fifteen, he left grammar school. With a friend, he began to sell wallpaper and other hardware supplies from a truck which they drove around markets in the small northern towns. But his life took an unexpected turn one day in a Manchester cinema. After buying his ticket, he discovered a Victorian coin among his change, a prototype which in its time had served as a model for minting. With his good business sense, he realized that this rare piece must have some value. He decided to take it to a numismatist (a coin specialist) who bought it from him for £4, which was not an insignificant sum at that time.

Cohen made a decision. He began to search for similar models of antique coins, buying and selling them, until he possessed one of the largest collections in Britain, almost comparable to that of King George VI. He stopped chasing after coins, however, when he met his future wife, Cherryl. She had come at her father's request to spend a summer internship in one of the first wallpaper and hardware stores established by Cohen. At the time she was only sixteen. He fell in love with her, and she in turn found herself attracted to this young, self-made man who concealed his sensitivity and intelligence beneath a tough veneer.

Her father, Jack Garson, was a respected merchant, and it was through him that Cohen discovered the

LEFT Seascape on the coffee table, Grayson Perry's vast *Emotional Landscape*, 1999. In front of this, a bronze sculpture by Antoni Tàpies, *Free* ('Libre'), 1984

ABOVE LEFT *Frank*, 2003/04, a sculpture of the collector by Tomoaki Suzuki.

ABOVE RIGHT Frank and Cherryl Cohen.

work of L. S. Lowry, a painter already well known outside his county of Lancashire. Seeing in Lowry an artist who realistically depicted working-class life in the north of England, Cohen began to collect prints by the artist: observations of factories at closing-time, textile mills, street scenes and above all ordinary people. The prices commanded by these works would increase considerably when, ten years later, people began offering them for sale at Christie's and Sotheby's.

Over time, Frank Cohen bought many works on paper and resold some of them at double or even triple their original prices. He also began to buy works by popular British artists such as Edward Burra, William Roberts, Kenneth Armitage and, of course, Lowry. But he remained somewhat constrained by the lack of specialized art venues in Manchester at that time. In fact, only one art gallery of quality offered an interesting selection, and he was compelled to criss-cross London's galleries in order to build a substantial collection of works.

Above all, the collector wanted to establish a personal connection to the figure hidden behind the objects he desired, and so he tracked down the reclusive Lowry. In the 1970s, he began to develop a craving for paintings and sculptures, not just works on paper. He already owned fifty-seven prints and drawings which were by their nature fragile, so Cohen decided to buy his first Lowry canvas: *My Family*, which reminded him of his own background.

One day, while he was walking in London's Cork Street, which is well known for its numerous galleries, he stopped in front of Leslie Waddington's gallery, where he was completely captivated by a painting on display in the window, by the American artist Jim Dine. He negotiated valiantly with the dealer, who recognized in Cowen a new and serious collector, allowing him to take the painting home without immediately paying for it. This was an inspired moment for the dealer, because Frank Cohen became one of his most faithful clients and would eventually buy a large number of works from him, including pieces by Jean Dubuffet, Joan Miró and Mimmo Palladino. Cohen had now entered the arena of international collectors, and had become someone to be taken seriously in the London art

ABOVE In the bedroom, above the bed, hangs Jim Dines's *4 Hearts Grain*, 1981.

RIGHT William Roberts's painting *Snooker*, 1968/69, dominates the study.

market. He continued to acquire works from the greatest dealers, including Crane Kalman from whom he bought numerous examples of modern British art, one of its most fertile and exciting periods. By the end of the 1980s, however, the most well-known and talented artists had become too expensive in Cohen's opinion, and he began to search for a new direction, discovering it in contemporary art.

At the beginning of the 1990s, the collector sold his company Glyn Webb, one of the most successful chains of DIY hardware stores. He now had at his disposal the financial means to increase his acquisitions, and consequently the pleasure they brought him. He decided to concentrate on the art of his time, and initially bought artworks by newcomers. However, he wanted to understand the evolution of the different artistic movements that were unfolding in the world, such as the new school of Dresden in which he had a particular interest. He amassed multiple works by the young Dirk Skreber, Andreas Slominski and many

others. As for the English, he purchased work by the Chapman Brothers, Damien Hirst, Tracy Emin, Martin Creed and David Shrigley – the 'Young British Artists'.

Frank Cohen is ever more passionate about his art. At the moment his entire collection can be found in a warehouse an hour and a half away from his home, right in the middle of the countryside. This first space was opened in order to store the pieces and to maintain his archives. Two people work there on a full-time basis to manage the collection, which attracts museum administrators and international collectors whom he welcomes personally.

Always open to special visitors, Cohen's home is worth the detour. Conceived jointly with his wife, who is similarly drawn to the pure minimalist architecture of Le Corbusier and Mies van der Rohe, this refined house adapts itself marvellously to the rather eclectic collection. The large Japanese garden provides shelter to numerous sculptures by an array of contemporary artists. Looking out of the kitchen window, you can just discern a gigantic sculpture by Mimmo Palladino, which blends into the greyness of the sky and serves as a watchman over the house. At the base of a Japanese

LEFT Amphibians on stilts next to the garden pond, Benedict Carpenter's *Green Frogs (series 3)*, 1999

ABOVE RIGHT In the garden, the wooden sculpture *The Ancestors* by Michael Dennis .

185

bridge, frogs seem to be pushing through the ground.

As his selections reveal, Frank Cohen is a man brimming with energy and enthusiasm. Today his collection consists of approximately one thousand works of art, leading him to establish a private foundation in Manchester, the FC MOCA, the first of its kind in this part of the country. Not only will the foundation exhibit artworks from the collection, it will also serve as a venue for shows by emerging artists. Working with Manchester City Council, he has developed a very ambitious programme for the site because he wants the British public, particularly people in the north, to enjoy and benefit from his collection. In the same spirit, an impressive educational programme is planned once the centre opens.

If Frank Cohen is called 'The Saatchi of the North', he has certainly earned his reputation as an audacious, tough and important collector who started out with nothing, and who even now remains strongly connected to his roots. This dedication has helped him to acquire a unique collection of art which he now intends to share with everyone.

Through everything, he has never lost the enthusiasm of his youth, nor his distinctive sense of humour, which he sometimes uses as a weapon. In fact 'funny' is his favourite word for describing the artworks he loves.

ABOVE Helmut Newton's book of photographs entitled *Sumo*, on a display stand by Philippe Starck.

RIGHT Art in front of a glass tile wall, (above) Charles LeDray's clothes stand *Chuck*, 1997, and (below) an untitled dog by Abigail Lane, 1999.

DOUBLE PAGE OVERLEAF View of the garden, (foreground left) Kenneth Armitage's *Figure lying on its side*, 1957, and (outside) William Turnbull's *Fin 2*, 1957.

Antoine de Galbert
TRACES OF AN EXISTENCE

Antoine de Galbert is an unassuming man, totally straightforward in his dealings with others, but at the same time extremely sophisticated. Born into a traditional aristocratic family from the French provinces, he is always ready to take a new look at himself, and possesses a critical intelligence that has nourished a wide-ranging collection, extending from ancient *objets d'art* to contemporary work by unknown young artists.

He lost his father when he was very young, and it was his aesthetically minded stepfather who awakened his passion for beautiful things. He grew up surrounded by fine furniture, carpets and old pictures, with the *Gazette de Drouot* permanently on the coffee table. After studying political science, he went to work as a young executive in commerce and distribution before he and his wife, a lawyer, decided that as soon as they had the means to do so, they would begin a new life. She became an actress and singer, and he opened what he now laughingly calls an 'art boutique', where he put on eclectic exhibitions of Art Brut, photographs and pictures

LEFT Lurking behind the door is John Isaacs's *Potatohead*. Hanging up is an Eskimo costume from North Alaska.

by contemporary artists both known and unknown. A resolute novice, he displayed what he liked, and even now in hindsight feels that he made very few mistakes in those early days, no doubt largely because he encountered a mentor who would pass on some of the basic secrets. Paul Gauzit, a dealer and collector from Lyons who sold modern, ancient and also primitive art, taught him above all to appreciate the universality of works and the concept of continuity in the history of art – a notion which he has adhered to throughout his time as a collector.

After opening a new gallery, on a larger scale than his first, but with the same emphasis on meeting people and forming friendships, he came to realize that commerce simply wasn't for him, so once again he decided to change his way of life. In 1999 he moved to Paris. Fickle? Let's just say that he is always on the move, and often becomes 'someone else', but he never forgets his priorities: his need to 'accumulate' works of art comes from a need to surround himself with things that 'reassure' him – especially contemporary art. Despite his purchase of works by such established names as Warhol, Rainer and Basquiat, he is an avid

191

supporter of contemporary art because he 'loves young artists'. His watchwords are 'be useful', 'live f or tomorrow', 'do research', and 'take part in this great human adventure': above all, he is drawn to living art and to particular trends.

Having entered the art world at a time when it was dominated by the Minimal and the Conceptual, he prefers new forms to abstract art, which he often finds boring. People can't change: he would like to be 'minimal', but his inner self resists, he says with a smile. He is not, however, a 'trendy' collector who simply follows fashion; he is more inclined to act on intuition when he visits the galleries and fairs, sometimes deciding in only thirty seconds, without even bothering to find out who the artist is. He has supreme faith in his own instincts regarding art, for his eye has undergone twenty years of training, and he considers the purchase of a work as the fruit of a visual culture and a strong subjective im pulse, akin to that of that of a hunter on the prowl.

ABOVE At the head of the bed is a photograph by Frank Mädler, 2000.

OPPOSITE The living room, with writing high up on the wall, a neon sign *You Are All Going to Die* (Vous allez tous mourir), by Claude Lévêque.

In Antoine de Galbert's collection there are works by Claude Lévêque, Pierrick Sorin, Markus Raetz and Zhang Huan. He acknowledges no hierarchy of genres, artists, or the media they use, because all that matters is their power to express something from the artist's time on earth. In this context, Art Brut, which he liked from the very beginning, runs as a kind of thread through his collection, which is permeated both with the idea of death and a certain scepticism, for behind all the cheerful bonhomie lies a complex character which is in harmony with the sensitivity and uncertainty of many artists. He too is certain of nothing. If he felt otherwise, he says, he would not collect.

His views on art will no doubt evolve, of course, but he hopes that he will always retain the spontaneity necessary to grasp the magic of art, which is equally potent in painting, sculpture and video, a medium that aroused his interest from the moment he found that he could make concrete images of his acquisitions by projecting them onto the wall above his fireplace. His house is tucked away in a popular quarter of Paris, where you would not expect to find such a sophisticated residence, and from where you can hear

the bells of a nearby church, which makes it seem
almost like living in a village. Here, the mixture of
genres is obligatory, and the colours and materials of
Morocco mingle with the most contemporary designs.
The large picture windows and verandas flood the
house with light, while a courtyard is converted into
a winter garden. Art is everywhere: pictures, videos,
modern sculptures, Art Brut and ancient objects all
blend together in discreet harmony where nothing
seems out of place. The house is just like the family
that inhabits it – dominated by a passion that is as
natural as everyday life.

It is scarcely surprising that Antoine de Galbert
wished to share his love of art with the general public
in the framework of a new foundation which has led
him deeper into research and exchanges with others.
La Maison Rouge - Fondation Antoine de Galbert
opened its doors in June 2004, in an old factory built
around a 19th-century residential lodge. This building
is divided into four
exhibition rooms as
well as conference rooms,
some of which have been
decorated by Jean-Michel Alberola, of whose work
Antoine de Galbert has been a consistent admirer.
There is also a lecture hall, bookshop and café.

Unusually, however, the purpose of this foundation
is not to house Antoine de Galbert's collection,
but to function as an art centre which will put on
temporary exhibitions based mainly on the theme of
private initiative, showing the relationship between
a collector and his or her works. This is the first centre
of its kind in France, which offers to as large a public
as possible access to international private collections,
alternating with thematic exhibitions and shows
devoted to a single artist, exchanges with foreign
museums, and last but by no means least a concerted
effort to promote installations by young artists.

If you ask him for the underlying meaning of all this
activity, he will answer simply that he is an heir, and he
sees it as his duty to do something both for the artists
and for the public; he wants to leave traces of his
existence by creating something worthwhile. Even if
collecting is utopian as well as a defence against death,
one thing is clear: although it may 'resolve nothing',
nevertheless it is as good a way as any of living one's life

LEFT An antique chest of drawers
with inlays.

ABOVE RIGHT Pierre Molinier's
La Jambe (The Leg).

195

by creating a work of one's own, or at least by trying to do so. At the age of forty-eight he does not know what will become of his collection, and he is not even sure that anyone would want to inherit such a mixture since it is so very private and individual. All the same, he is obviously attached to the idea of passing it on, and it is difficult not to regard him as a kind of model, even with all his excesses. Of these he remarks with a twinkle in his eye that he has reached the limits of obsession, but what he does not say – once more out of modesty – is that his kind of obsession also gives pleasure to everyone else.

ABOVE LEFT Tribal art from New Guinea.

ABOVE RIGHT A Yoruba costume from Nigeria.

OPPOSITE Mathilde de Galbert's room.

DOUBLE PAGE OVERLEAF The room is dominated by Gilbert and George's massive *Street Beached*, 1991. In the foreground is a table by Hans Wegner, and on this is a Bambara animal head from Mali.

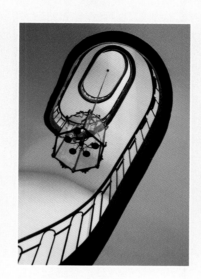

Gilbert Brownstone
AN AMERICAN IN PARIS

Gilbert Brownstone has never chosen the easy route. It needed an American in Paris, courageous, analytical, passionate, intuitive, to do battle on behalf of Minimal art, and to make it known to a reluctant French public. He fought with every means at his disposal, trying one approach after another, through museums, galleries, catalogues, books, and finally through his own private foundation. Curator, dealer, writer and collector, he has amassed one of the largest collections of Minimal art in France, and within the framework of his foundation has even sent it across the Atlantic in order to reveal this highly demanding form to American art lovers.

Gilbert Brownstone and his wife Catherine have nevertheless chosen to spend most of their time in Paris, in a 17th-century apartment that is typical of the Marais district, full of charm and history, which one reaches by climbing a beautiful staircase that bears the footsteps of the centuries. In their world, the past blends harmoniously with the present. Photographs by Seton Smith and Philippe Ramette fit in splendidly with the antique curtains, and the parquet flooring is reflected in a Haim Steinbach sculpture, on which the artist placed some carafes bought from the Tour d'Argent in Paris, while Gilbert Brownstone himself has added a bottle of *Château Cheval Blanc* in readiness for his guests. When the collector acquired this work, Steinbach was delighted that its new owner was taking it back to Paris, where it first saw the light of day. Over the fireplace in the living room are analytical drawings by Masson, acquired when Gilbert was living with the artist, and when one sits in the patent-leather armchairs so wonderfully conducive to relaxation and cogitation, one has a piece by Claude Rutault on one side and an Isabelle Waternaux photograph on the other.

The living room leads to a sober but welcoming room that is decorated with just one painting, by Callum Innes, representing fireballs descending after a firework display – perhaps a metaphor for love. The Brownstones appreciate works that make you think, but they pass easily from serious contemplation to laughter, and from reflection to action.

LEFT A peep into the bedroom. Above the bed hangs *A Thousand and One Nights – Fez* (Les milles et une nuits – Fez), 1975, by Erró.

ABOVE RIGHT Catherine and Gilbert Brownstone. In the background is Philippe Ramette's photograph *Pedestals for reflection (utilization)* (Socles à réflexion [utilisation]), 1989-2002.

ABOVE LEFT The staircase seen from below.

It was in 1990 that Catherine Bret, journalist and chief fashion editor for *Vogue France*, entered the life of Gilbert Brownstone, together with her two children (he also has two of his own). Like him she loved art, and when they were not too busy in their ever-changing world, she made some fine ceramics herself. Together they met many artists and began to surround themselves with works that were very different from those that Gilbert had previously owned. The reason was simple: when the American got to know the Frenchwoman, their extraordinary compatibility gave him far more than any of his pictures could, but he still found a certain comfort in the contemplative spirituality of Minimal and Concrete art. He was a friend of Honneger, whose monochromes had a soothing effect. This new love and harmony naturally led the Brownstones towards a new vision of life.

Gilbert's tastes underwent a transformation, and he shared Catherine's passion for photography. With her, he started a new collection that included photographers such as Seton Smith and Isabelle Waternaux, and artists such as Philippe Mayaux, Philippe Ramette and the Cuban Capote brothers. In this spirit of renewal, he gave his entire collection of Minimal and Concrete art to the Norton Museum in West Palm Beach in the United States, where they spent a good deal of their time. Thus the seventy works remained close to them, while the museum itself benefited from a valuable and inspired collection that extended from Josef Albers to Olivier Mosset, and included Honneger, Fontana, Soto, Richter, Imi Knoebel, Sol LeWitt, John Armleder, Franz Erhard-Walther, Ed Ruscha and Jean-Pierre Raynaud.

Gilbert Brownstone was born in New York in 1938, and studied political science and art history in Paris, which should have launched him into a career as a museum curator. He went back to the States in 1963, and for the next four years he worked at the Federation of Arts, where he met Louise Nevelson, with whom he remained friends until she died. Following this, from 1967 to 1973, he was mainly occupied with the beginnings of the ARC (Animation-Recherche-Création), the progressive contemporary art

ABOVE Philippe Ramette's *Untitled (In Praise of Laziness)* (Sans titre [Eloge de la Paresse]), 2000, leans in a corner.

OPPOSITE Behind the sofa is a large colour photograph by Isabelle Waternaux from the series *Stillness, Untitled* (Sans titre), 1999.

department of the Musée d'Art Moderne de la Ville de Paris, where he worked alongside Pierre Gaudibert and the present director Suzanne Pagé. He threw himself wholeheartedly into this project, more as the 'animator' of a creative centre than as a *conservateur* in the literal sense of the word.

During the mid 1970s, after a brief spell as director of the Picasso Museum in Antibes, where he felt too constrained, he was invited in 1973 by Wilhem Sandberg to be his successor as curator of the Israel Museum in Jerusalem. One of his main duties was to build up the permanent collection, and he divided his time between Israel, France and the United States. After a few years, however, he decided to go back to France, and so he left for Antibes to give himself the chance to think and write. It was then that he made up his mind to abandon his career as a museum curator, which he would certainly have been able to continue in the United States if he had wanted to, but at the expense of his family life and his children.

Nevertheless, he recalls, 'There was nothing else I could do except work in the arts.'

He therefore decided to open a gallery in Paris, which he did in 1985: Brownstone et Cie, rue St Gilles, in the heart of the Marais district. There he simply represented the artists whom he liked and who really made him think, especially American and European Abstract and Minimalist artists such as Honneger, Judd and Klein, who were not yet recognized by the French public, and also Jean-Pierre Raynaud, Imi Knoebel, Gerwald Rockenshaub, Olivier Mosset, Sylvie Fleury, Ed Ruscha and Claude Rutault. For nearly ten years, Gilbert Brownstone enthusiastically promoted this essentially difficult art, winning the trust of his artists and his friends, who followed him faithfully through this artistic adventure.

'When I was working in museums,' he remembers with a laugh, 'the artists always asked me, "Did many people come and see the exhibition? How did the press react, and the other museums?" But when I did the same work in a gallery, the artists never asked me those questions. In fact, my artists were very patient with me because they didn't regard me as a shopkeeper. And yet

205

what artists want a gallery owner to do is sell their works!' He feels that the artists he has helped have been so kind to him because they know at heart how much he loves art and how hard he always worked for them when he was a curator. In 1999, however, he decided to put an end to his career as a gallery owner in order to devote himself to opening an American foundation in Paris, which would give him greater freedom of action.

The Brownstone Foundation opened its doors in 2000, with the aim of promoting contemporary art and artists in all creative fields, from the plastic arts to choreography, and spreading the influence of French art by organizing international exchanges, particularly through agents.

Gilbert Brownstone, who has already published his own views on contemporary art, recently brought out a stimulating book entitled *La Chair et Dieu* (Flesh and God), published by Albin Michel, a thought-provoking dialogue between the Church and contemporary artists such as Andres Serrano, Marina Abramovic and Boris Mikhailov. The author himself acts as host and mediator in an exchange between enlightened representatives of the ecclesiastical world and a form of art which he passionately wants the public to react to and reflect on, in the light of the world's problems, the misery of humankind, and the way in which these are depicted in contemporary art.

Catherine and Gilbert Brownstone have a shared view of the present, of life, the world as it is and of the future. Art is always there, surrounding them and bearing witness to all of this and to their own constantly renewed passion. Are they just collectors? It would be true to say rather that they are active lovers of the arts and supporters of artists.

ABOVE Ivan Capote's sculpture made from shells and a thin iron rod, *Untitled* (Sans titre), 2000.

OPPOSITE Esko Männikkös, *Gina and Natividad, Batesville*, 1997.

DOUBLE PAGE OVERLEAF Simple design – a desk by Le Corbusier and chair by Jean Prouvé. Above is a cibachrome by Seton Smith, *24 interiors*, 1993.

Hubert Neumann
LOVE AND CERTAINTY

When you visit Hubert Neumann's home on Riverside Drive in New York City, you feel as though you are entering Ali Baba's cave, a veritable labyrinth covering four levels, each filled from floor to ceiling with extraordinary works of art. Your eye is immediately drawn to a wall hanging – an assemblage of letters and postcards addressed to his father, Norman Neumann, accompanied by various photographs – and you can make out the progression of signatures from artists such as Dubuffet and Léger.

LEFT Every inch is covered with art. At the back is Chuck Close's *Susan*, 1971, flanked by two Jeff Koons sculptures. In the foreground, *Woman's Head* (Tête de Femme) by Picasso, 1939, is leaning against a plinth, and in the centre lies a figure by the French artist Xavier Veilhan.

ABOVE LEFT To the left, on the wall, is a picture by Jean-Michel Basquiat, and in the foreground, a picture and sculpture by the Venezuelan artist Meyer Vaisman.

DOUBLE PAGE OVERLEAF A quiet corner with DIY: a cupboard with sixteen circular saws and three gas canisters by Wim Delvoye, 1990. On the opposite wall is a Basquiat, *Untitled (Tyranny)*, 1982.

The rooms in the lower level are devoted to contemporary and to more classical works, all arranged as though they had just been delivered, some still wrapped up or in their crates. In the centre sits Hubert Neumann's desk, piled high with papers, belying the fact that he is actually very orderly and meticulous.

Works by the contemporary American artist Karen Kilimnick can be found everywhere but particularly in the dining room, accompanied by delicacies from Claes Oldenburg. On the staircase leading to the upper floor, walls are adorned with engravings and canvases by Picasso, Dubuffet, Magritte, Ernst, with more pieces by Karen Kilimnick and Christian Schumann. Different periods and styles are combined. On the landing, a dignified American grandmother by Duane Hanson greets you, standing on top of a work by Carl Andre, and in front of an enormous canvas by Lichtenstein. The living-room floor is papered with books and documents. Covered in dust, Giacometti's sculpture of a dog stands in contrast to nearby works by Warhol and Picasso. It is easy to find artistic exchanges throughout Neumann's home: here, on an upper floor, a Chuck Close talks with a Jeff Koons, while elsewhere a Miró confronts a Franz Kline and a Xavier Veilhan. Just like the rest of the house, Hubert and his companion's bedroom offers no Zen-like sanctuary. Picasso's *Owl* and Giacometti's *Annette* watch over their sleep as though they were preventing the little figures in Christian Schumann's canvases from waking them!

Born in Chicago at the beginning of the Second World War, Neumann pursued a career in business. His reputation is that of a man who says what he thinks and whose ideas on life and art are very specific; but he is also known for his deep humanity and commitment to young artists whom he defends passionately. Initiated into the world of art by his father, he quickly began to develop his eye, the key attribute of the most audacious collectors. And although he was not always able to buy what he loved, he began his life as a conoisseur by collecting books, porcelain and silver *objets d'art*.

Becoming more successful and influential after the war, Neumann's father travelled to Europe for the first time with his family and, during a trip to Paris in 1952, they met Léger, Dubuffet, Daniel-Henry Kahnweiler, and the art dealer Denise René. 'My father,' said Neumann, 'had this incredible instinct for meeting fantastic people,' acquiring works by Giacometti, Miró, Picasso, Matisse and Cubists such as Juan Gris as well as pieces by other modernists which were

ABOVE Graffitti: Keith Haring's large painting *Untitled (Dancing Dogs)*, 1982.

OPPOSITE Above the staircase hangs a mobile by Alexander Calder, *Untitled, exec., c.* 1950.

still affordable at that time. His father was far more attentive to the quality of the particular pieces that he bought, rather than the artist's reputation. Learning at his side, Hubert Neumann served both as witness and accomplice to his father's discoveries and, at the beginning of the 1950s, when he was barely in his twenties, he began to involve himself fully in the enrichment and enlargement of what would become, little by little, their own collection.

In 1954, Hubert moved to New York which had by then replaced Paris as the centre for international art. He visited galleries, exhibitions and artists' studios with his father, engaging in long conversations with him about the path of their growing collection. American abstract art aroused their interest in particular, especially after they visited the studio of the young Franz Kline. Completely seduced by a large canvas, 2 m (6 ft) high, which the artist had only just finished, they purchased it on the spot, rolled it up and passed it through the studio window directly into their car.

Unusually in a family, the tastes and choices of this father and son team evolved in the same direction and at the same pace. They changed their outlook with each

period, eager to discover new artists and new trends and always ready to embark on a new course, leaving behind well-trodden aesthetic paths. From 1962 onwards, they put their trust in the emerging young Pop artists, understanding that 'when you bought the work of a young artist, it was a true emotional commitment. Oftentimes people who look at your selections think that they are terrible! Therefore you need to be completely sure of the pieces you choose and of your feelings towards them so as not to be thrown off balance. It is not an easy thing,' concludes Neumann.

For this connoisseur, falling in love with an artwork remains the driving force in a collection which never adhered to a clear stylistic agenda or a chronological construction. For example, even after they turned towards Pop Art, if a lovely Miró presented itself, the Neumanns gladly purchased it. Always on the look-out for great works, they also became passionate about Photorealism. Hubert adored this influential movement. He and his father discovered Chuck Close quite by accident

ABOVE Next to the sliding door sits Duane Hanson's deceptively realistic *Woman with Suitcases*, 1973; to the left is Roy Lichtenstein's martial *Live Ammo*, 1962.

during a gallery visit when he was almost unknown.

After his father's death, Neumann centered his collection around Postmodernism, guided naturally by his interest in Chuck Close and the Photorealist movement which essentially gave rise to it. In order to love Postmodernism, according to Hubert, you had to be sensitive to everything that was happening in the contemporary world, but also to be aware of how art had developed, with new currents being built on older foundations. In this respect, he lamented that Postmodernism did not have greater support, attributing the reserve which greeted the movement to the art world's need for landmarks: it still clung desperately to the style which had defined its era and tried to prolong and expand the idea of Modernism.

In contrast, it has always been more important for Neumann to be on the threshold of discovering new approaches, and he playfully bemoans the fact that he does not encounter this interest in the new frequently enough among contemporary institutions and collectors. Partly, no doubt, because 'there is much money in play in the world of art that the milieu is very conservative and feels the need for security, which

therefore makes it wary of any innovation which could revitalize it and render it more dynamic.' Happily though, he recalls, there were still dealers around who were still totally involved in their work and choices.

True to his convictions, he has not shied away from playing the role of Maecenas to new artists such as the young French Postmodernist Xavier Veilhan, even developing with him the piece presented by the artist at the 2003 Lyons Biennial, the fruit of a genuine collaboration which became a real friendship over a period of several years. In this work the public entered an installation consisting of a large wooden cube with a shadowy interior (like a photographer's darkroom), covered over with an opaque plastic material. Photorealist tableaux from Hubert Neumann's collections were recessed in the walls and lit only by slender beams of light, a little like windows opening onto scenes of American life.

Every work in Hubert Neumann's collection fundamentally represents a personal commitment to human experience as translated through the perspective of an artist, and it is this engagement which forms the magical relationship between the works which interest him, not just on an intellectual level, but above all on an emotional one. In his world, it is impossible to miss the multiple connections between the works of living artists and those of the past masters. He maintains that 'when Basquiat was twenty-two years old, his works had to rub shoulders with Picasso's,' and so Hubert hung their paintings opposite each other.

We could add that it is this same youthful spirit that leads him into an unfamiliar gallery, trusting his instincts. Thanks to this spontaneity, his collection has grown through a series of unexpected encounters, such as the day when he walked into a gallery and found a young man painting an enormous tableau in the basement. Hubert asked him to reserve the work for him when it was finished. The young man was none other than Jean-Michel Basquiat. No one in the art world knew who he was then or had any idea of what he would shortly become. Their history together began that day for the artist, his collector and for his family who are also interested in art.

ABOVE Right from the start, Hubert Neumann's father acquired classic works of modern art: paintings (top row, from left to right) by Juan Gris, Picasso, Paul Klee and Fernand Léger. On the bench below one can see a wrapped newspaper by Christo, in front of which is a metal sculpture by Jeff Koons.

217

Two of Hubert Neumann's three daughters have
become passionate art lovers, clearly understanding
the humanist role that art has played for their father.
In this respect, he has brought others round to his
approach, and has used his charisma and talent to
convince numerous collectors and friends to move to
the forefront of artistic exploration. He has converted
his entourage to Postmodernism and has, above all, left
this moving message: there is nothing more important
in a civilization than its works of art, because art reflects
the very highest levels of human activity. The need to
create has existed since the dawn of time, and Hubert
Neumann is continuing the long and important
tradition of providing support for artists, passing
on his beliefs and passions
from one generation to
the next.

Frederick R. Weisman and Billie Milam Weisman
THE AMERICAN DREAM

Frederick R. Weisman fulfilled the American dream. The son of an immigrant Russian furrier, his life was one of brilliance and courage, and he never deviated from a steadfast spirit of scepticism that was also part of his charm. His foundation, which since his death in 1994 has been run by his widow Billie Milam, is the living proof of his insatiable curiosity and lust for life. These basic qualities contributed to one of the most important American collections, tracing the development of 20th-century artistic movements from the east to the west coast of the United States, with particular emphasis on art in California, where Frederick Weisman first became successful.

It was his pioneering spirit that enabled him to make his fortune by gaining exclusive rights to import Japanese Toyota cars into America, at a time when they were not yet fashionable. He could certainly have rested on his Japanese laurels, but Frederick Weisman was a man with a lively,

questioning mind that juggled with lots of good ideas at the same time, and furthermore put them all into operation. His legacy is that of an inspired, demanding man who was quite capable of ringing his colleagues in the middle of the night in order to discuss a project close to his heart. Nevertheless, he was also cautious in the sense that he would never trust the judgment of just one person, but would always seek confirmation from several. Only then would he draw up his plans, and from that moment on, nothing could stop him from implementing them to the full.

He became a 'golden boy' in his field, and in the late 1940s he began collecting with his first wife Marcia, who was the sister of the great collector Norton Simon. At that time in the United States, if you had the will and talent, you could rise rapidly up the social ladder. Frederick and Marcia took full advantage of this climate and decided to add an artistic touch by collecting artworks, partly following their own tastes, but also seeking advice from specialists, including the New York art dealer Ben Heller. Thus they built up a very fine collection of modern French works, later augmented by post-war American abstract artists such

223

as Clyfford Still, Franz Kline and Morris Louis, but also including works by Picasso and Max Ernst. They enjoyed meeting and forming relationships with the artists, followed their progress closely, and helped them by buying their art. For example, they purchased three of Clyfford Still's major pieces, and this enabled him to buy a farm which he converted into a studio.

Frederick R. Weisman and Billie Milam became a couple in the early 1980s, although she had already been working for him over a period of time as an adviser for his collection. She was then curator at the County Museum of Art in Los Angeles as well as at the J. Paul Getty Museum. Having always been deeply involved in art, Billie had studied art history at the University of California before becoming a curator at Harvard, thereby entering the world of museums. When she was in her twenties, she bought her first pre-Columbian artworks which, with their abstract

purity, fitted in perfectly with Frederick's modern, contemporary collection.

When they first met, she was immensely impressed by his exceptional eye and artistic intuition, as well as by his experience as a collector. In turn, this dynamic and enthusiastic woman, always full of ideas, lively, fashionable, with sparkling eyes yet a modest demeanour, fascinated Frederick. She likes to say self-effacingly that he certainly influenced her view of art more than she influenced his; but what he gave her above all was the liberty and confidence to trust in her own instincts and her individual approach to art. For Frederick, having the means to acquire works of art was a blessing which he believed it was his duty to share. It was as if the businessman had bound himself to a social contract, and it seemed to him self-evident that he must give something back to the world, the public, the artists and everyone else who had helped him to achieve his success. This was the main reason why he set up his foundation in 1982.

He converted his main residence into a living museum for his friends and close relatives, but in the same spirit he also decided to send his works on a grand

tour, organizing exhibitions in the United States, Europe and Asia, including some of the most remote places where people would normally never have a chance to see modern and contemporary art. Through his foundation he also set up a programme to finance museums and to make loans and gifts of his works.

Once the foundation was established, Frederick and Billie continued to acquire more works. They decided to promote Californian art, and supported artists such as John Baldessari, Ed Ruscha, Robert Irwin and Joe Goode. Frederick wanted the world to know that there was a genuine Californian school just as there was a New York school and so, when he offered to finance a contemporary wing at the Pepperdine Museum in California, he made it clear to the curator that so long as he presented the entire Californian collection, the wing would be his; but if he did not do so, Frederick would take it back!

He was already involved in financing the Museum of Californian Art in San Diego, a wing of the Museum of Contemporary Art in New Orleans, and the Museum of the University of Minnesota and Minneapolis, which was designed by Frank Gehry: in its originality it is considered to be a precursor of the museum in Bilbao. Frederick regarded it as part of his mission to promote radical and unrecognized contemporary art, and this was also part of his own need to keep developing in line with his time. Both he and Billie remained close friends with those artists whose work they had acquired, and she has continued to fulfil the task of helping those creative spirits whom she believes to be 'the conscience of our society' and 'bearers of our soul'.

Today, Billie Milam Weisman devotes most of her time to art and to carrying on the work of her late husband. Just like Frederick, she is intent on preserving the integrity of his collection in the same spirit that gave rise to it in the first place. She is just as conscious as he was of a collector's duties, for she knows how beneficial and fundamental the role of a patron is in a country like the United States, where the government offers no real support for contemporary art. On a daily

ABOVE In Frederick R. Weisman's former study, Duane Hanson's deceptively realistic sculptures of the collector and his mother Mary Weisman. Behind them are pictures by Josef Albers (left) and Hans Hofmann. On the right is a bronze sculpture by Magritte, *The Gioconda* (La Joconde), 1967.

OPPOSITE On the table is Yves Klein's *Blue Venus* (Vénus Bleue), 1961, and behind it a screen in matching colours, *Remember and forget*, 1986, by Ed Ruscha.

basis she fosters the relationships that the foundation has built up with museums, particularly with regard to the loan of works, and she makes it a point of honour to continue organizing touring exhibitions, studios, lectures and any educational activity that might bring American children into the museums and art galleries.

The foundation is now open to the public by appointment, and the collection has been preserved exactly as the Weismans first installed it. It was important to Frederick that visitors should see his works in a more welcoming atmosphere than is usually found in most museums, that they should experience them in the same way as the collectors themselves, in intimate proximity to the pieces around them.

The villa itself is in a Mediterranean style, and was

LEFT Max Ernst's bronze sculpture *Moonmad*, 1956, seems to be presiding over the conference table. In front of it is Naum Gabos's *Linear Construction 4 Variation 2* (Construction linéaire 4 Variation 2), 1963. On the wood-panelled wall hang two prime pieces of Surrealism: *Il trovatore*, 1926, by Giorgio de Chirico on the left, and *Le chef d'oeuvre ou les mystères de l'horizon*, 1955, by René Magritte on the right.

designed by Gordon B. Kaufman. It is typical of Beverly Hills, and has a huge terraced garden. Visitors can gaze on monumental works by Botéro, Henry Moore and Allen Jones. While

the interior is relatively classical, the picture windows allow in plenty of light and create a link with the exterior, although the true originality of the building lies in its contents. Art is everywhere, even in the tiniest details. The walls are covered with fascinating works, right down to the magnificent panelling of Frederick's office, where you will find paintings by Hans Hofmann, Jasper Johns, Willem de Kooning and Kenneth Noland, as well as sculptures of his parents by Duane Hanson. In one corner is a double portrait of Frederick by Andy Warhol. The furniture too – tables, chairs and sofas – is decorated with sculptures by Yves Klein and Jose de Rivera, and the living room is stuffed to the ceiling with artworks. Suspended above the bar in the music room is a gigantic geometrical relief by Ronald Davis, while in the bathroom you will discover Billie Milam Weisman reclining in the form of a life-size sculptured portrait. Adjoining the main house is another building, designed by the great Californian architect Franklin Israel, with a room that houses the largest items in the collection.

All of this contributes to the foundation's success, and for Billie it is living proof that art is a fundamental

ABOVE The breakfast room,
with table and chairs by Bjørn
Wiinblad. The cake is a work by
Claes Oldenburg. 1964.

OPPOSITE Larry Rivers's *Beauty
and the beasts*, 1975, reaches
up to the ceiling (right). In the
corner is a sculpture by John
Buck. Yves Klein's version of
Nike of Samothrace stands on
the grand piano, and behind it
is Kenneth Noland's painting
Prime course, 1964.

part of being human, that nothing is too good for it. Thus she continues the campaign by acquiring more works, focusing particularly on young American artists, but also on some Europeans. She travels a lot, as she used to do with Frederick, and goes on discovering, marvelling and improving herself and the world through her contact with art. As she says herself, it's a kind of therapy: 'You go out, you look at works, and they cleanse your mind and your soul. When you have seen art, you are better placed to take decisions, and probably take more humane decisions as a result.'

LEFT A synthetic resin sculpture by Luis Jiminez ploughs the garden, *Sodbuster San Isidro*, 1984.

OVERLEAF LEFT A neon installation by Alice Lees is reflected in the pool: *Caryatides descending*, 1986; to the right are two bronze figures by Tom Otterness. The ceramic disc on the pillar to the left, next to the Ionic column, is by Peter Voulkos.

OVERLEAF RIGHT Surrounded by flowers, George Segal's bronze sculpture *Rush Hour*, 1983-84, is modelled on Rodin's famous *The Burghers of Calais* (Les bourgeois de Calais), 1884-86.

Acknowledgments

My special thanks go to AXA Art, Germany and The
Art Document Company, Netherlands.

I would also like to thank the following people for their
skill and support: Inge Rodenstock, Marina Aarts,
Toula Ballas, Guy Boyer, Fréderic B. Brand, David
Brolliet, Dan Bronner, Tobias Christ, Pieter C. W. M.
Dreesmann, Robin Fournier-Bergmann, Sabine
Gludowacz, Matt Green, Johnny van Haeften,
Anthony van Hagen, Stefan Horsthemke, Carl Kostyal,
Laurence Bertrand d'Orléac, Gilles Marcellier,
Christian Muller, James Neal, Catherine Nell, Norman
Rosenthal, Monique Scholten-Klinkenberg, Catherine
Tanazacq, Nathalie Varga, Margit and Rolf Weinberg,
John Winter, and Philippe Wright.
Thanks also to everyone else who has helped us to
make this project a reality.
Bomann-Museum, Stiftung Miniaturensammlung
Tansey, Celle, Germany (www.bomann-museum.de)
Clos Pegase Winery, Shrem Sculpture Collection,
Calistoga Valley, USA (www.clospegase.com)

Collections open to the public

Deste Foundation – Centre for Contemporary Art,
Dakis Joannou Collection, Athens (www.deste.gr)
Fondation Pierre Bergé et Yves Saint Laurent, Paris
(www.ysl-hautecouture.com)
Gilbert Brownstone Foundation, Palm Beach, USA
Frederick R. Weisman Art Foundation, Los Angeles,
USA (www.weismanfoundation.org)
Hamburger Bahnhof – Museum für Gegenwart, Marx
Collection, Berlin (www.smb.spk-berlin.de)
La Maison Rouge, Antoine de Galbert Collection,
Paris (www.lamaisonrouge.org)
Phoenix-Kulturstiftung, Falckenberg Collection,
Hamburg-Harburg
Goetz Collection, Munich (www.sammlung-goetz.de)
Olbricht Collection, Folkwangmuseum, Essen
(www.museumfolkwang.de)
Rosengart Collection, Lucerne, Switzerland
(www.rosengart.ch)
Villa di Celle Sculpture Garden, Gori Collection,
Santomato di Pistoia, Italy

Picture credits

Picture credits: page 2: 20 porcelain figures *Obsessive Memories* (2003) by Liu Jianhua in the house of Uli and Rita Sigg; pages 4–5: eagle sculpture *Grande volo* (1961) by Quinto Ghermandi in Giuliano Gori's park; page 6: Ben Vautier's *No more art* (1985) in Hubert Neumann's house.

First published in the United Kingdom 2005 by Thames & Hudson Ltd, 181A High Holborn, London WC1V 7QX

www.thamesandhudson.com

Translated from French and German by David Wilson Essays on Cohen, Dreesmann, Neumann and Shrem translated by Toulas Ballas

Original edition © 2005 KnesebeckGmbH & Co. Verlags KG, Munich
A Company of La Martinière Groupe

British Library Cataloguing-in-Publication Data
A catalogue record for this book is available from the British Library

ISBN-13: 978-0-500-51256-2
ISBN-10: 0-500-51256-6

Printed and bound in Germany